GW00459139

The DUCHESS HORTENSE

Hortense Mancini Duchesse Mazarin by Pierre Mignard

The
DUCHESS
HORTENSE

Cardinal Mazarin's Wanton Niece

BRYAN BEVAN

The Rubicon Press

The Rubicon Press Limited
57 Cornwall Gardens
London SW7 4BE

British Library Cataloguing in Publication Data

Bevan, Bryan
    The Duchess Hortense : Cardinal Mazarin's
    wanton niece.
    1. Mancini, Hortense 2. Courts and
    courtiers —— Europe —— Biography
    I. Title
    940.2'2'0924   D274.M3/

    ISBN 0-948695-07-2

Designed and typeset by The Rubicon Press
Printed and bound by Biddles Limited of Guildford and King's Lynn.

Contents

Acknowledgements

To the late Cyril Hughes Hartmann, whose book *The Vagabond Duchess* (1926) inspired me to write my own work.

To the London Library for their constant help and for allowing me to keep works long after the permitted period.

To the Director and Staff of L'Institut Français for their help.

To the Hon. Victor Montagu for allowing me to use the fine Pierre Mignard of Hortense Mancini on the jacket.

To Mrs. Colville of 11 Kensington Square for her kindness in showing me round her delightful home.

To my friend Andrew Low for his help in sundry ways.

To my sister Winfreda Murray for helping me with proofs and index.

To my publishers Anthea Page and Juanita Homan of The Rubicon Press for their helpfulness and courtesy.

List of Illustrations

Introduction

Our Victorian forebears regarded with horror the sexual behaviour and antics at the Courts of Charles II and his cousin Louis XIV of France during the latter part of the seventeenth century. One wonders, however, whether the prevailing immorality has not been somewhat exaggerated. It is at least arguable whether Charles's Court was more unlicensed than various others known in history. To understand the behaviour of the courtiers one must bear in mind that it signified a protest and revolt against the puritanism of Commonwealth England. Many of the cavaliers in exile had been strongly influenced by their experiences in France and the United Provinces, their enforced idleness, their struggles against penury and their natural craving for amusement and variety as an escape from the monotony of their lives.

Both Hortense Mancini and her sister Marie were before their time in their whole attitude towards sex. Italians by birth, they were brought up at the Court of the young Louis XIV in France. Their contemporaries considered them very unconventional and their behaviour inexplicable in defying popular opinion and running away from their husbands despite gross provocation. They were not so much criticized for taking lovers - that was the usual practice in their circle - as for their outrageous conduct. Even their own sisters Olympe Comtesse de Soissons and Marianne Duchesse de Bouillon, both unfaithful wives, who at the time of Hortense's and Marie's flight were established at the head of fashionable Parisian society, declared not without spite and certainly without charity that they were behaving like madwomen and ought to be seized and imprisoned.

It is extremely likely that Hortense's and Marie's dislike of convention and their refusal to conform partly owed their origin to their uncle Cardinal Mazarin's very strict, harsh treatment of them in the early days at the court of Le Roi Soleil. Their hatred of constraint and their love of freedom are more reminiscent of a

1

woman living in the late twentieth century than one living three centuries earlier. In the flush of their youth and indeed throughout their lives they pined for self-expression and freedom like prisoners gasping for air. Yet it is notable that none of the Mancini sisters gave themselves to king or commoner before marriage.

The Mancini sisters, Olympe, Marie, Hortense and Marianne deliberately flouted the conventions of their age. Laure their eldest sister died too young, a virtuous girl naturally sweet and charitable, whose arranged marriage to the Duc de Mercoeur proved harmonious. After Laure's death, her disconsolate husband sought solace in religion eventually becoming a cardinal and Papal Legate in France.

In their restlessness and craving for liberty, Hortense and Marie may well have been subconsciously influenced by Queen Christina of Sweden, a brilliant but unstable woman. She abdicated her kingdom in 1654, no longer able to tolerate the restrictions, responsibilities and duties of monarchy. Hortense was only a little girl of about eleven when the Queen, a lover of France, visited Compiègne, perceiving with her acute intelligence that Louis was very much attracted to Marie. She gave the King of France some welcome advice: "If I were you I'd marry somebody I loved." It meant nothing to her that Louis for state reasons had to marry a suitable wife. If he loved Marie, why not marry her? And the little Hortense would be told how Christina with her masculine voice liked to dress like a man, wear masculine gloves and even a man's wig. She was undoubtedly a lesbian.

It is curious that Hortense, so essentially feminine (unlike Christina) should have a liking on her adventurous journeys, to wear breeches like a man and even a periwig, but a kind of disguise was necessary when escaping from her husband the Duc Mazarin. Again later in her strange career, about to embark on a dangerous journey to England, taking her through Alsace, Switzerland and Germany, she bravely donned the dress of a cavalier, and "befeathered and bewigged" rode on her way, triumphing over every obstacle.

In this permissive age with its violence and much publicized sex abuse we are more hardened and less inclined to condemn too rigorously the licentiousness at Charles II's court. Whatever we may think of the rakes and debauchees such as John Wilmot Second Earl of Rochester, George Villiers Second Duke of Buckingham and Sir Charles Sedley the poet, father of a celebrated mistress of James Duke of York, it cannot be denied that "the merry gang" as Andrew Marvell called them, were men of wide culture and literary ability. Rochester, son of Henry Wilmot, a boon companion of King Charles during his escape after Worcester, was a lyrical poet of genius, inspired by his wife and his most important mistress, the actress Elizabeth Barry. Despite his licentiousness and depravity he managed to write poetry of haunting originality. Sir George Etherege in his play *Sir Fopling Flutter* or *The Man of Mode* created a character Dorimant, modelled exactly on his friend Rochester. 'I know he is a Devil, but he has something of the Angel yet underfaced in him.' Rochester touched the heights and the depths, the puritan at war with the sensualist in his complex character. Hortense Mazarin's friend Seigneur de St. Evrémond wrote: "Rochester was generally fickle in his amours, and made no great scruple of his oaths of fidelity." We know later that Lady Sandwich, the daughter of the boon companion of Charles II, Rochester frequently attended Hortense's parties in her apartments at St. James's.

Buckingham, a dissolute friend of the Duchesse Mazarin, wrote a play called *The Rehearsal*, a veiled attack on Dryden, best known as the work from which Sheridan took his play *The Critic*. When Buckingham, a great nobleman, mortally wounded the Earl of Shrewsbury, the husband of his mistress Anna Maria in a duel, there was considerable scandal, but Buckingham hardly cared a jot what his wife felt. Charles on the other hand very much disapproved of duels, but he eventually pardoned Buckingham. There was a public outcry, however, when Buckingham wanted to have his illegitimate son by Lady Shrewsbury christened in Westminster Abbey. It is curious how profligacy may be more consistent with genuine talent and genius than virtue.

At the same time there were many virtuous women in the late seventeenth century, such as Hortense's Martinozzi cousin Mary Beatrice Duchess of York (a future Queen), Dorothy Osborne, the wife of the accomplished diplomatist Sir William Temple, a writer of exquisite love letters as well as Charles II's

3

own illegitimate daughter, "his Charlotte" Countess of Lichfield, as chaste, strange to say, as her mother the Duchess of Cleveland was wanton.

The punishment for ordinary people was extremely severe, even brutal. It was not unknown for a man or a woman to be whipped at the cart's tail for sexual offences or for vagrancy. Flogging was freely resorted to. Anthony à Wood relates several sordid cases where 'in the middle of this month a maid and a dog were hang'd at Tyburne for that the dog laid with her severall times.'[1] No mercy was usually granted to people of humble birth. Anthony à Wood relates a harrowing story (December 14th 1650):

> "One Anne Green a servant maid, was hang'd in the Castle of Oxon, for murdering her bastard-child, begotten by Jeffry Reade grand-son to Sir Thomas Read of Dunsten in Oxfordshire. After she had suffer'd the law, she was cut downe, and carried away in order to be anatomiz'd by some young physitians, but they finding life in her, would not venter upon her, only so farr, as to recover her life." It is pleasing to know that despite her terrible injuries she eventually recovered.[2]

Anthony à Wood relates another macabre case (May 4th 1658) where a maid was hanged at Greenditch (now St. Margaret's Road where the city gallows stood) "for murdering her infant-bastard. After shee was cut downe and taken away to be anatomiz'd William Coniers (Conyers) a physitian of St. John's Coll. & other young physitians, did in short time bring life into her. But the baillives of the towne hearing of it, they went between 12 and one of the clock at night to the house where she laid and putting her into a coffin carried her into Broken hayes, & by a halter about her neck hung her on a tree there. She then was so sensible of what they were about to do, that she said, 'Lord have mercy upon me' etc. The women were exceedingly enraged at it, cut downe the tree whereon she was hang'd and gave very ill language to Henry Mallory one of the baillives when they saw him passing the streets" . . . When he later failed in his trade as a cutler and became impoverished people said that God's judgement follow'd

4

him for the cruelty he shew'd to the poor maid. These grisly events occurred during the Commonwealth, but they are typical of others during the Restoration. I only record them to emphasize the stark contrast between the lives of the aristocrats and wealthy citizens often able to escape the results of their misdeeds and the poor and defenceless. The squalor, the violence, the dirt were abundant and, above all, the beauty. Kensington and Chelsea were still villages, while Knightsbridge, Wandsworth, Islington and Paddington remained mere hamlets. There were, however, vile districts where the sober citizen rarely penetrated, such as the district stretching from the Temple to Blackfriars known as Alsatia, a name with a sinister and evil association, for robbers and other criminals flourished there. The most fashionable districts lay in Covent Garden, but many others were in Southwark or Bankside.

There was undoubtedly one law for the rich and those with influential friends and another for the poor. Count John Königsmarck, a Swedish nobleman and chief instigator of the dastardly murder of Thomas Thynne of Longleat (Tom o' ten thousand), a great friend of the Duke of Monmouth, in St. Alban Street off Pall Mall in February 1682, almost certainly owed his release to the intercession of Charles II, though his underlings went to the gallows. Thynne had made a forced marriage with a young and wealthy widow Lady Elizabeth Ogle, the daughter of Josselyn Percy eleventh earl of Northumberland, and Königsmarck had coveted the lady also, having been one of her earlier suitors.

Peers wanting to rid themselves of unfaithful wives occasionally took their cases to the House of Lords. Having obtained a separation in the spiritual courts, Lord Roos in a celebrated case during 1669 succeeded in obtaining a civil divorce, but a special Act of Parliament had to be passed as he wanted to remarry.[3] Charles II attended some of the debates, saying that it was as entertaining as going to the theatre. Plagued for many years by an adulterous wife, the Duke of Norfolk during 1690 - William and Mary had jointly succeeded to the throne - was forced to commence proceedings in the House of Lords for his marriage to be dissolved because of the adultery of his wife Mary with Sir John Germain, a coarse courtier of Dutch extraction. The evidence of one of the witnesses in the State Trial, a Mrs. Benskin, a servant of the Norfolks, is very interesting because of various allusions to Nell Gwyn. When Germain had tried to persuade Nell to sleep with him (Charles II had died in 1685), Nell had cheekily told the Duchess "that she could not lay the dog where the deer laid, for she knew My Lady Duchess would accept of him".[4] Less fortunate than Lord Roos, Norfolk was compelled to wait until 1700 before obtaining an Act of Parliament sanctioning his divorce.

No sexual scandal during the later seventeenth century in England could compare with the grotesque horror and iniquity of L'Affaire des Poisons in Louis XIV's France during 1680. The age of this great king was, perhaps, the most glorious in French history, but Louis rightly feared that the scandals unearthed by the Royal Chamber of the Arsenal, better known as the *Chambre Ardente*, the 'burning chamber', would sully his *gloire*. Even the famous Racine was accused of having murdered an actress, while the king's mistress Madame de Montespan was deeply implicated in profane acts of sacrilege and black magic.

The reputation of Hortense's sisters Olympe Comtesse de Soissons and Marianne Duchesse de Bouillon suffered as a result of their involvement in this terrible affair. Louis probably believed in Olympe's guilt - he knew her intimately - but he would have been wiser to have confined her in the Bastille, for she was suspected of poisoning her husband, instead of giving her the alternative of exile abroad in the Spanish Netherlands. His worst mistake was to stir up the resentment of her son Prince Eugène of Savoy, thus making a formidable enemy of an eminent soldier, destined to fight with deadly success against Louis's armies in the ensuing years.

6

CHAPTER I

The Cardinal's Nieces

The Mancini sisters, nieces of Louis XIV's great Minister Jules Mazarin, were among the most fascinating, notorious and illustrious ladies of the later seventeenth century. Hortense, always his favourite, possessed superb Italianate beauty, but throughout most her life of forty-five years she was completely amoral, despite her devoted admirer Saint-Evrémond's later assertion: "With the beauty of ancient Greece, Hortense combined the virtue of ancient Rome." He was writing of her after she became the Duchesse Mazarin.

Hortense was born in Rome in 1645, fourth daughter of Cardinal Mazarin's sister Jeronima and her husband Lorenzo Mancini, a Roman gentleman and gifted amateur astrologer, who could trace his ancestry back to the fourteenth century. Mazarin also made an excellent match for his elder sister Margarita, marrying her to Girolano Martinozzi. Their daughter Laure was to make a brilliant marriage with Alphonso, fourth Duke d'Este, thus becoming the mother of a future Queen of England, Maria di Modena.

Jeronima had a large family by Lorenzo Mancini, three sons, Paul, Alphonse and Philippe and five daughters, Laure, Olympe, Marie, Hortense and Marianne.

It is timely to say something about Hortense's uncle, Cardinal Jules Mazarin, a statesman of immense ability, an Italian by birth who served France with devotion. His father Pietro Mazarini came from Palermo in Sicily, being much indebted to the patronage of the Constable Colonna, one of the great nobles of Italy. His mother Hortensia Bufalini came of good Umbrian nobility. To escape the heat of Rome she went to Piscina in the Abruzzi where she gave birth to Giulio (July 14th 1602).

Mazarini's early diplomatic training was acquired in the service of the Holy See, but strange as it might seem when he left the Roman College of Jesuits he had the reputation of a profligate

7

gambler. Certainly his travels to the Courts of Madrid, Turin, Mantua and Paris gave him a taste for luxury and beautiful things. In his early career, Giulio Mazarini knew Spain very well, and spoke the language fluently. He tells us, however, that it was a servant of the Duke of Parma, who predicted that all his future advantages and honours would accrue to him from France and so it proved. At first distrusted by Cardinal Richelieu Louis XIII's minister, it was not long before Richelieu divined young Giulio's innate ability, recommending him when dying. The King gave him employment, creating him 'The Minister of State'.

Olivier d'Ormesson a contemporary described Mazarin as "Tall, of good appearance, a handsome man with chestnut hair, lively and amused eyes, and a great sweetness in his face."

His resemblance to Charles I's favourite George Villiers, first Duke of Buckingham, who had once tried to make love to Louis XIII's Spanish-born Queen Anne of Austria (Philip IV's sister), may have influenced Anne to favour him. As he is the dominating influence in the early lives of his nieces his own personal life is of interest. Too much credence must not be given to the statement of Charlotte Elizabeth of Bavaria, second wife of Philippe (Louis XIV's brother), for she wrote in 1717 long after Mazarin's death: "The widow of Louis XIII did much more than love Cardinal Mazarin,[1] she married him." When aged fifty-nine Anne wrote him "To the last breath Anne is yours, whatever you may believe."

It is very unlikely, however, that Anne of Austria was either his lover or secretly married him. The Duchesse de Chevreuse, a great friend, told Cardinal de Retz that there was nothing between them but a liaison of the mind. Although deferential to her in the early days, he was capable of treating her in a rude, off-hand manner. Madame de Brienne, one of her ladies-in-waiting, alarmed lest her royal mistress was deceiving her, was bold enough to enquire of her what her real feelings for the Cardinal were. Anne told her, and there is no reason to believe her insincere: "I grant you that I like him, and I may even say tenderly, but the affection I bear him does not go so far as love, or if it does so without my knowledge it is not my senses which are involved but only my mind, which is charmed by the beauty of his." She might be extremely flirtatious, but she possessed a great deal of Habsburg pride.Religious by temperament, and fastidious too, even prudish, such a woman is unlikely to have had sexual relations with the Cardinal, who in any case once had aspirations to be Pope. Anne lived constantly in the public eye. Even her women of the bedchamber slept at the foot of her bed.

Though Mazarin possessed the Italian art of pleasing, he was much disliked at Court, being hated by the people of Paris as a foreigner. His chief fault was his avarice.

The young Louis XIV scarcely a boy succeeded to a troubled kingdom on the death of his father (1643). France was torn by civil war, the Wars of the Fronde. On two occasions Mazarin was compelled to seek refuge abroad, pursued by the malice of his enemies the Frondeurs with their bitter Satires:

> 'Adieu, donc, pauvre Mazarin
> Adieu, mon pauvre Tabarin;
> Adieu, *l'oncle aux Mazarinettes*,' . . .

He stayed at Bruhl near Cologne where his eldest Mancini niece Laure made a brilliant marriage with the Duc de Mercoeur, a grandson of Henri IV and his beautiful mistress Gabrielle d'Estrées; Laure died early much to the grief of her husband, who became a priest and later a cardinal of the Holy See in France.

There is no doubt that Mazarin exploited the charms of his nieces for his own ends, anxious to arrange influential marriages for them so that he might thereby gain powerful connections. Though he might feign indifference,[2] the clever Cardinal knew that their arrival in France would strengthen his position. Hortense relates that she was only six when she first came to France, but she was in fact removed there in 1653 aged eight together with her elder sister Marie by their mother Madame Mancini, a woman of harsh, unpleasant character. Her contemporaries said she was ill-tempered, bigoted and certainly extremely superstitious. Her husband had warned her in one of his prophetic moods, saying that Marie would only bring disasters on people connected with her. As a child Marie, unlike Hortense, gave no indication that she would develop into a charming and vivacious girl. Thinking she was only fit for a convent, Madame Mancini early influenced her brother against Marie. Her special favourites were Hortense, probably because of her beauty, and little waspish Marianne, who early revealed a precocious wit.

When the Mancini sisters were first presented at Court to the Regent Queen Anne of Austria, the wife of Maréchal de Villeroi remarked shrewdly to Gaston d'Orléans, Louis XIV's treacherous uncle: "See those little girls, who are now not rich; they will soon have fine châteaux, large incomes, splendid jewels, beautiful silver and perhaps great dignities." At first, however, Madame Mancini was given apartments in the Louvre in Paris, and Marie and Hortense shared her life. Her antipathy to Marie was so marked that she soon persuaded her brother the Cardinal to send her to the Convent of the Visitation in the Faubourg St. Jacques, to be joined two months later by little Hortense. Mazarin, though enchanted by Hortense's beauty, became uneasily aware that the whole Court was spoiling her excessively, particularly Philippe, Louis XIV's younger brother, who swore that he could not live without her.

While her sister Marie, the most studious, clever and intellectual of the Mancinis, was revealing considerable aptitude for learning and talent for French literature and Italian poetry, Hortense aged nine took the opportunity at the beginning of July 1654 to write to her uncle to remind him that she had not received her promised pocket money. "I intended to wait till I was better at writing, but I am become impatient to know if little Hortense is still honoured with your remembrance . . . It would be the summit of my happiness if Your Excellency would favour me with a visit, as you have promised me; if I cannot have that honour, at least I very humbly beg Your Eminence to remember to give orders to Monsieur Colbert[3] touching that which you have promised me every month for my diversion and for giving alms to the poor"; . . . Hortense, like all her sisters, stood in considerable awe of her uncle, but she regarded him with little affection, though she ended one of her letters "May God keep you in health while I try my best not to forfeit the honour I bear of being your very humble niece and servant who loves you with all her heart," signed Hortense de Mancini.

With Mazarin's triumphal return from exile after the Wars of the Fronde, his position as Louis XIV's Chief Minister virtually be-

10

came impregnable. He was deeply saddened, however, by the early deaths of two of his Mancini nephews, Paul and Alphonse. Paul was killed aged fifteen whilst fighting bravely as a royalist officer during the Wars of the Fronde, while Alphonse, a studious boy, to whom Mazarin was deeply attached, fractured his skull owing to the stupid antics of his fellow pupils, who were tossing him in a blanket. For his surviving nephew Philippe, Mazarin always evinced a marked aversion, despising his frivolity and indolence, though he was amiable enough. This favourite brother of Hortense won the esteem of Louis XIV, who appointed him Captain of his Company of Musketeers. Serving as Lieutenant in the same company was the Comte d'Artagnan, hero of Alexandre Dumas's romance. Disapproving of some youthful escapade in which Philippe was implicated, Mazarin had him imprisoned for a time in the citadel of Brussac.

Hortense's sister Olympe resembled her uncle in character in some respects more than any of her sisters. She had a similar love of ostentation and a notorious partiality for intrigue, but she was ambitious, indiscreet and vindictive, and the Cardinal with his brilliant intellect was certainly neither indiscreet nor vengeful. In his early life Louis XIV who had been brought up with her, was much attracted to Mlle. Olympe, and the affair was much discussed at Court. Her uncle regarded it in a tolerant way, but for a moment his ambition may have been tempted.[4] No evidence, however, exists that Louis at seventeen thought of Olympe as a possible Queen. Indeed the Cardinal had once offered both Olympe and Marie in marriage to Armand de la Porte, Marquis de la Meilleraye, an extremely wealthy nobleman, not of very illustrious lineage. In declining the honour of marrying Olympe, Armand tactlessly told the Cardinal that if he married at all it would be for his salvation, but a marriage to Olympe would be merely "justement le grand Chemin de la Damnation". There he showed a certain shrewdness.

The Marquis de la Meilleraye was one of those young men, who fall passionately in love in youth and never waver in their allegiance. Armand first fell desperately in love with Hortense, then a child of ten, at a ball given by Monsieur (aged fifteen) at the Palais Royale in 1655. To such an extent was he smitten that he told others that if he could not marry Hortense he would enter a monastery. If only he could achieve his wish, he would gladly die three months later.[5] On his part the Cardinal was very angry, declaring (according to Hortense's Mémoires) that he would prefer to marry her to one of his own lackeys. As for Hortense merely a child, she was amused at the Marquis de la Meilleraye's ardent adoration.

Poets raved about her loveliness. Loret in his *Muse Historique* describes her at a Court ball:

> 'La Mignonne Hortense
> Qui parut dans ce noble bal
> Comme un jeune astre oriental.'

Louis XIV was very fond of Hortense, though he once told his mother that he did not like little girls, referring to his cousin Henriette d'Angleterre.[6]

During 1657 the Cardinal arranged a brilliant marriage for Olympe with Prince Eugène de Savoie-Carignan, and henceforward Olympe and her husband were treated as of the blood royal. However, as the title of Comte de Soissons was revived for her husband, she was usually referred to as Comtesse de Soissons or at Court as Madame la Comtesse. There are indications that once married Olympe was quite ready to grant the young King her favours. She would entertain him lavishly at the Hôtel de Soissons, but she later became aware that Louis came there to visit her sister Marie rather than herself, for Marie had matured into a charming and vivacious girl. Olympe, jealous and vindictive, wanted to prevent any chance of the romance maturing.

Hortense was very close to Marie in her early life, and she became her chief confidante in her love affair with King Louis. After her mother's death (1656), Marie was much at Court. She might lack Hortense's classic beauty, but she was extremely attractive with large expressive black eyes, fine teeth, her hair jet black, her figure supple and becoming. The romance, however, only slowly developed. While the Court was at Calais during April 1658 - he was now nineteen - Louis fell desperately ill with fever and almost died. The fickle courtiers as is their way were ready to desert him for his younger brother Philippe. On his recovery, however, Louis

12

was informed of Marie's incessant tears and her genuine grief at the prospect of losing him.

So there grew in the heart of the young king a love, which gradually became a consuming passion. According to Mademoiselle de Montpensier Louis's first cousin, the king was never gayer and better-tempered than when he was in love with Marie Mancini.[7] She mentions Olympe "by no means showing the grief that she should have shown". At nineteen he was a callow youth, knowing little of life or love and dependant on his mother or the Cardinal. Louis indeed owed much to Marie. She was the first to perceive the latent greatness in the young king. She imbued him with noble ambitions and confidence in himself, frankly scolding him for his ignorance and giving him a taste for learning. Far more than is realised Louis owes his later title of "Le Grand Monarque" to Marie's on the whole beneficial influence. Yet it was unwise of the tactless, capricious girl to go out of her way to disparage her uncle, who already disliked her, even ridiculed her, fearing her influence with the king. She even criticized the Queen-mother. Nevertheless one can argue that she was the most romantic and emotional passion of Louis's life. She possessed a kingly interest in kingly things and politics interested her.

So deeply did Marie love Louis that she was constantly exhorting Hortense, a girl of thirteen, to fall in love. Hortense admits that "being extreme young and childish" she did not obey her sister's behest. Her uncle bade her governess Madame de Venel, devoted to his interests and wholly in his confidence and prepared to spy on her charges, to catechize Hortense about her supposed admirers, but the governess failed to make any discoveries. Perhaps more to please Marie than for any other reason, she at length admitted that she looked with much favour upon a young Italian lieutenant in the Guards. Marie repeated this to the King and it soon came to the Cardinal's ears. When the young man emboldened by Hortense's alleged infatuation for him began to make advances, Hortense according to her Mémoires rejected them with disdain. Whether Hortense's account is truthful or not is doubtful because she was always inclined to embellish or distort what happened in her life. Her most persistent admirer was the Marquis de la Meilleraye, who continued to send her love-letters, but she took no notice of them. Hortense later reproached herself for not being sufficiently sympathetic to Marie over her love for Louis.

She wrote in her Mémoires "The things which passion makes us do, seem ridiculous to those who have never known what passion is."

Hortense was aged about fourteen when the exiled and penniless Charles II of England asked Cardinal Mazarin for her hand in marriage. Charles's intermediary in this affair was his trusted adviser the Abbé Walter Montagu, who wrote to the Cardinal (December 20th 1659): "The request I have to make to you for my master is that you will not promise your niece Hortense in marriage to anybody until I have had the honour of speaking to you."[8]

Queen Henrietta Maria, Charles's mother, was also eager for the match because of the enormous dowry Hortense might expect from Mazarin. However, during the Commonwealth the wily Cardinal had formed an intimate alliance (1654) with Cromwell. He was wrongly convinced that Charles would never regain his throne. This was his real reason for declining the match. Diplomatically he told Montagu that Charles must not think of honouring his niece while Louis XIV's first cousin Mademoiselle de Montpensier remained unmarried. An insincere excuse because the Cardinal was well aware that the lady had not the slightest intention to marry Charles.[9]

In her Mémoires Hortense relates an amusing story about her youngest sister Marianne, though it shows neither the Cardinal nor Queen Anne in a favourable light. Marianne was a gay amusing little creature, a great favourite of Anne of Austria's for she had a real gift for writing verse. On his part Mazarin liked to tease Marianne then aged six about her pretended beaux. He even went so far as to reproach her for being with child, but Marianne hotly protested on being provoked. According to Hortense, one fine morning Marianne woke up to find between her sheets a newly born baby. "You cannot imagine the astonishment and the grief she felt at this sight." "Only the Virgin and I have experienced this," she said. The Queen came to console her, and wanted to be godmother (Marraine). When pressed to tell the Court the name of the father, Marianne declared: "It can be no one but the King or the Comte de Guiche, because they are the only men who have ever kissed me." Hortense, who was only three years older than Marianne, was all agog (toute glorieuse) to ascertain the truth of the matter.[10]

Marianne's waspish, slightly spiteful rhymed letters, so eagerly read by the Cardinal and the Queen, sometimes contained sly digs at Hortense. She was quite certain that Hortense would never learn to dance well.

> "Parce qu'elle n'a pas la patience
> De retenir sa grosse panse (belly)"

When Anne of Austria gave all the Mancini sisters watches as presents, Marianne could not resist telling her uncle that Hortense has had the finest watch of us all, though the four were exactly similar except for their colour.

The Summer of 1658 was the happiest period in Marie Mancini's chequered life. She was virtually a queen and all the festivities at Fontainebleau, the comedies and ballets, water-parties on the lake and informal picnics in the woods were organized in her honour. The King and Marie basked in the present, having little thought for tomorrow. In her Mémoires Marie relates a delightful incident, vividly depicting Louis's gallantry. They were walking fairly quickly amidst an alley of trees at Bois-le-Vicomte when Louis, wishing to take her hand, accidentally bruised her with the hilt of his sword. Whereupon with a charming gesture he drew it from its sheath and threw it away. Such an action endeared him all the more to her romantic spirit. As for Louis he was infatuated with Marie and wanted to marry her.

Gradually her uncle the Cardinal came to realize that the affair was serious. Far from encouraging Marie to pursue her romance, Mazarin became deeply apprehensive, knowing that Marie disliked him personally. As for Queen Anne, she could hardly conceal her aversion. Madame de Motteville, however, in a celebrated passage [11] insinuated that the Cardinal was a slave of ambition, with an innate desire to prefer his own interests to those of anybody else. Laughing at the folly of his niece, he mentioned her desire to marry the King to the Queen-Mother. Anne then exclaimed, "I do not believe, Monsieur the Cardinal, that the King could be capable of such baseness; but if it were possible that he should think of it, I warn you that all France will revolt against you and him, and that I will put myself àt the head of the rebels, and induce my second son (Philippe Duc d'Anjou) to join them." Now Madame de Motteville rather disliked the Cardinal, and may well have invented this conversation. It is doubtful whether the Queen would ever speak to Mazarin in such a way. His massive correspondence reveals that he greatly distrusted his niece, aware that he had no sort of ascendancy over her, and fearing that if she were to become Queen of France, he would be relegated to the background. He knew her·passionate, headstrong character. Furthermore, for reasons of state, Mazarin was determined to negotiate a marriage between King Louis and a Spanish Infanta, since this was the only way to achieve an enduring peace after twenty years of war. So, far from favouring any possible marriage of the King with Marie, he strongly opposed it.

It was an adroit stroke to negotiate a possible marriage between Louis and Princess Margarita of Savoy, but Mazarin never intended the negotiations to succeed. His own purpose was to force Philip IV of Spain (Anne of Austria's brother) to make an offer of his own daughter Maria Theresa to King Louis. The Court, including Marie and Hortense, travelled to Lyons that Autumn (1658) to meet the royal family of Savoy. It was there that a special envoy Pimentel arrived incognito from Spain with the offer of peace and the hand of the Infanta. Mazarin was cautiously optimistic and Anne of Austria overjoyed. At first Louis seemed to find Princess Margarita attractive, but he paid far more attention to Marie Mancini, who was overheard by La Grande Mademoiselle to say to the King: "Are you not ashamed, Sire, at their wishing to give you so ugly a wife?" Much to the distress of the Duchess of Savoy, the proposed marriage came to nothing. Young Charles-Emmanuel Duke of Savoy, Margarita's brother, impressed by Hortense's beauty whilst in Lyons, began negotiations to marry her, but he asked for the fortress of Pignerol belonging to France to be included as one of the conditions of the marriage. Mazarin refused this request and the negotiations broke down. It may well be that Charles-Emmanuel, a suitable parti for Hortense, was incensed by the shabby treatment given his sister.

16

Whilst in Lyons Marie and Hortense were lodged in the Place Bellecour. When the Cardinal heard that the King and Marie were constantly together in the Place Bellecour on moonlight nights he expressed great uneasiness. Instead of supping with his mother, Louis preferred to converse with Marie, while Hortense gambled, being assisted in keeping the bank by her steadfast admirer the Marquis de la Meilleraye. The Cardinal charged his faithful satellite Madame de Venel to keep the closest watch on her and her sisters. Hortense relates an amusing incident:

> "Madame de Venel was so accustomed to her profession of guardian (or rather of spy), even at night, that she rose in her sleep to see what we were doing. One night, as my sister Marie lay asleep, with her mouth open, Madame de Venel, coming all asleep, as she was, to grope in the dark, happened to thrust her finger into her mouth so far, that my sister, starting out of her sleep, made her teeth meet in the lady's finger. My sister was extremely angry at this inquisition."

Next day, the story was related to the King and all the Court laughed over it. On one occasion when Louis was distributing sweetmeats to the ladies of the Court, Madame de Venel opened her box and to her horror a dozen mice ran out of it. It is likely that Marie suggested this to Louis.

When the Court left Lyons for Paris at the end of January (1659) Hortense, since she disliked the cold, went by coach with Madame de Venel while the Cardinal and the jealous Olympe travelled by water as far as Nevers. Marie, however, dressed in a black velvet jerkin and a bonnet trimmed with feathers, with a sense of freedom, wild elation and infinite joy, rode by Louis's side while a few younger courtiers kept a respectful distance from the lovers.

Convinced that Marie had a strong influence over Hortense, Mazarin wrote to Madame de Venel (August 18th 1659):

> "It is with great displeasure that I see she is involving Hortense in all her plans, but I am not surprised because my niece will have persuaded her that if she falls in with her wishes, she

will secure a brilliant future for her, and as Hortense is still a child, she must take this for gospel truth."[12]

Madame de Venel, however, considered that the Cardinal exaggerated Marie's hold over her sister. "Your Eminence can make her (Hortense) do what you like, when she sees that you are really angry," she wrote him. Her governess disapproved of Hortense because she used rouge.

Mazarin now resolved to travel South to discuss the negotiations for peace with Spain with Philip IV's plenipotentiary Don Luis de Haro. The proposed marriage with the Infanta became more than a possibility. Vowing that he would never marry her, the passionate young Louis went on his knees before his mother and the Cardinal, declaring that he was going to marry Marie Mancini, the only woman he could ever love. He ardently wanted the match because he could find no more striking reward for Mazarin's long and important services.

Madame de Motteville relates what followed. As the Queen's confidante she was undoubtedly well informed. Taking a torch, which was on a table, Anne of Austria asked her son to accompany her to her private apartments. It was an agonizing interview lasting an hour, in the course of which Anne used every possible argument against the marriage appealing to his sense of duty and honour. She feared a new kind of Fronde, a civil war. The King left with his face inflamed and tears pouring down his cheeks. The Queen murmured *sotta voce* to Madame de Motteville that the King would thank her one day for the wrong she was doing him.

As for the Cardinal he remained absolutely inflexible, declaring that he was deeply honoured by the King's regard for his niece, but refusing to allow him to make her his Queen. He proposed to remove Marie, Hortense and Marianne to La Rochelle on the Poitevin Coast in the care of their governess. Reluctantly he gave permission for the lovers to write each other. They would be allowed an interview at Bayonne.

Hortense tells of Marie's despair and of the unhappiness of the King. It so happened that Queen Henrietta Maria, much impoverished, had been recently obliged to sell a magnificent pearl necklace. Hearing of this Louis asked the Cardinal for 78,000 livres

18

so that he could present the jewels to Marie. Overcoming his customary avarice the Minister agreed to this. She was to cherish Louis's present all her life. It was on June 22nd 1659, a tragic day, that Louis and Marie parted. We know Marie Mancini's proud words, full of tenderness and passion, but with a touch of scorn and reproach: "Sire, vous êtes roi, vous pleurez et je pars." Giving way to her grief as she threw herself back in her couch and sobbing bitterly as she murmured to Hortense, "Ah, I am abandoned."

Hortense relates in her Mémoires that when the King and Marie met at Saint-Jean-d'Angely "nothing could match the passion displayed by the King or the tenderness with which he begged Marie's forgiveness for all she had suffered because of him."[13] Hortense was only a child, and she thought there was no reason why the King should not marry Marie. She felt bewildered, sympathizing with her sister, but unable to be of much comfort to her. She admired Christina the ex-Queen of Sweden, who on her earlier visit to France when seeing the lovers together, had said in her deep hoarse voice to Louis, "You should marry her."

Mazarin engrossed in delicate negotiations with the Spanish Foreign Minister for Louis's marriage to the Infanta bitterly reproached Louis. "You spend your time reading her letters (Marie's) and writing your own. What defeats my comprehension is that you resort to every imaginable expedient to inflame your passion when you are on the eve of being married." His strong criticism of Marie only inflamed Louis's passion, made him more obstinate. "She is inordinately ambitious," wrote Mazarin, "contrary and quick-tempered, despises everybody, behaves without restraint and is prepared for every kind of excess . . . In fact you know as well as I that she has a thousand failings and not a single quality that might make her worthy of the honour of your good will."[14]

It is very unfortunate that no letters from Louis to Marie survive, nor any from her to the King. Indeed their prolonged and enforced separation was to lead to terrible misunderstandings.

When Mazarin heard that Marie and Hortense spent considerable time at the desolate port of Brouage consulting a Moorish astrologer, who was teaching them astrology, he wrote sharply to Madame de Venel:

"If my niece (Marie) wants to know her future, her true
horoscope, I will tell you in one word. If she does not be-
have as I wish, she will be the most unhappy person in the
world."

Louis and Marie still desperately hoped that some impediment
would occur to prevent the King's marriage to the Infanta: when
Marie realized that their hopes were doomed, she determined to
cease all communication with the King. Intensely proud by nature,
it was all or nothing for her. The role of royal mistress would
never have satisfied her. Marie was forced to renounce Louis.

Meanwhile, Hortense's ardent suitor, the Marquis de la Meilleraye, known as Le Grand Maître, was as attentive as ever, constantly
visiting her at Brouage and trying to curry favour with Marie and
Marianne by sending them all sorts of presents, such as a marvellous
talking parrot, gold-mounted walking-sticks and half a dozen pairs
of Spanish gloves to Marianne, despite her complaints to the Cardinal that de la Meilleraye only wrote to her to ask news of Hortense.

After the Restoration of Charles II (May 29th 1660), Hortense's possible marriage to the King of England was again revived.
Mazarin, who had refused overtures during the Commonwealth,
now hastened to offer a magnificent dowry of 20,000,000 livres.
Charles, whether attracted by Hortense's fortune or by her beauty,
or more likely by both, may well have wanted the match, but Sir
Edward Hyde (soon to be created Earl of Clarendon) opposed it
on the grounds that it would be inconsistent with Charles's dignity
to marry a lady who had been refused to him during the days of
his exile. Hyde, too, was well aware of English sentiment towards
the French and the prevalent anxiety lest France should interfere
in English affairs. Hortense had many suitors, including a Prince of
Portugal, who was to succeed his brother as Pedro II and the elderly
illustrious soldier Marshal de Turenne. However, Turenne did not
press his claims, having the sense to realize that his age was an
impediment hardly making him an attractive husband for the
lovely Hortense.

The Peace of the Pyrenees had been negotiated by Cardinal
Mazarin and Louis had married Maria Theresa at St. Jean-de-Luz

during June 1660, but his longing for Marie Mancini obsessed his mind and separation could not alter her feelings for him. So, much to the consternation of the Cardinal and Queen Anne, instead of returning directly to Paris, Louis insisted on making a sentimental pilgrimage to Brouage, together with Marie's brother Philippe and a few favoured courtiers. He slept in Marie's bed in the château and went on long solitary walks along the lonely sea-shore, intending no doubt that Philippe would write his sister the King's reactions. Marie was now back in the Louvre.

For some time Mazarin had been considering a suitable marriage for Marie. It was essential for her to leave France, particularly since signs of the King's passion were only too clear. Remembering, perhaps, his father's association with the Colonna family in Rome, the Cardinal favoured the claims of Lorenzo Colonna, Principe Palliano and Grand Constable of the Kingdom of Naples, one of the greatest noblemen of Italy and Spain, but Marie did not want to leave her beloved France. She suggested another suitor, a Frenchman, Prince Charles of Lorraine, and her uncle, intent on the Colonna marriage, pretended to consider it. Marie, however, declared herself strongly against going to Rome.

With the connivance of Olympe, Comtesse de Soissons, who had never forgiven Marie for supplanting her in the King's affections and the Queen-Mother Anne, Mazarin devised a diabolical plot. Their intention was to play on Louis's pride and jealousy by falsely asserting that Marie had too willingly encouraged the advances of Prince Charles of Lorraine, having found consolation in her new-found love for him. Olympe took a fiendish delight in recounting to the King her sister's walks and alleged tender discussions in the Tuileries, not omitting to hurt Marie by informing her of her own relations with Louis. In reality Louis's image lay in her heart, and the wound was just as deep.

By July 13th the Court had arrived at Fontainebleau and Mazarin hastened to order his nieces Hortense, Marie and Marianne, to go there to pay their respects to the Queen-Mother. Marie Thérèse, only interested in food and Court etiquette, was not present, having postponed all formal receptions until after her entry into Paris.

When Marie, acutely agitated and embarrassed, presented herself before the King, she involuntarily raised her eyes, to be greeted with the greatest disdain and coldness.[15] Hortense in her Mémoires, confirms Marie's own account, writing that Louis's hauteur and apparent changed attitude made her decide after all to marry the Prince Colonna in Italy. Olympe, seeing her sister's desperate sadness, could not resist saying, "It must be very dull for you so far from Paris. I expect you miss your lover (Prince Charles)." "Perhaps I do," replied Marie, coldly and proudly, and Louis was within ear-shot as she spoke. Only to Hortense could Marie unburden her mind in the privacy of her apartments, free at last to indulge her passionate grief, and to complain of Olympe and the Queen-Mother.

Hortense relates in her Mémoires: "She would often pray me to tell her as many ill things of the King as I could." Hortense could give her little comfort except her sympathy:

> "It was rather difficult to speak ill of such a prince as he, who lived among us with a charming sweetness and familiarity, my age which was then only twelve (in reality she was fifteen) did not permit me to quite understand what was required of me, and all that I could do to help her, stricken with grief and loving her tenderly, was to weep for her misfortunes with her, until she might bear me company in weeping for mine."

Aged fifteen, Hortense was completely bewitching, with her enormous eyes, whose colour, between blue and grey, seemed to change with her moods. She possessed masses of blue-black hair, a face of Italianate classic loveliness, and a sensual mouth. There was a suggestion of wildness and originality about her.

Hortense, Marie and Marianne were present in the Hôtel de Beauvais in the mediaeval Rue François-Miron to see a glittering spectacle, the entry of the Queen Marie Thérèse into Paris. There they were joined by the Cardinal, Queen Anne, Queen Henrietta of England and the Princess Henriette, sixteen years of age, soon to marry the King's brother Monsieur. For Marie the spectacle was torture. How she suffered! Instead of this insignificant Queen, so insipid and colourless, her gown glittering with precious stones, it might be me, thought Marie. She almost heard Louis's voice, warm and ardent, "My Queen," he would say, "I will take no other woman."

During January 1661, just two months before his death, Cardinal Mazarin had an important interview with the Bishop of Fréjus to whom de la Meilleraye had offered fifty thousand crowns provided he could persuade the Cardinal to give him Hortense's hand. At last Mazarin agreed to the match, stipulating that the young man must take the title of Duc Mazarin, so that the Cardinal's name might be perpetuated. He would share her fortune of twenty-eight million livres and inherit the Palais Mazarin with all its wonderful works of art. It seemed to many of Hortense's contemporaries that de la Meilleraye, Grand Master of the Art-illery, Marshal of France, Governor of Alsace, Bourbon, Brittany and Vincennes, was a most desirable match. However his own father, knowing the fatal defects in his son's character, warned the Cardinal to no avail that it was far from desirable to leave his son so much wealth. Hortense was content enough to marry her faithful suitor, more interested in her pecuniary fortune than any sentiment for her husband. Hortense, who was completely irres-ponsible, relates that after her marriage, she and her sisters stood at a window of the Palais Mazarin throwing more than three hundred louis to the lacqueys below, richly amused as they scram-bled for the money. Hortense's extravagance and the divagations of the Cardinal's nieces may well have shortened his miserly life.

We get a picture of the Cardinal at his last evening party, in the Palais Mazarin, surrounded by the works of the great masters, Bernini, Van Dyck, Claude and Michelangelo. Heavily scented, with his pet monkey on his shoulder - all the Mancinis loved animals - he moves uneasily among his glittering guests, aware that he is generally disliked while concealed orchestras play Monte-verdi's exquisite music. Young Mademoiselle de Tonnay-Charente (later Madame de Montespan) heard him murmur: "To think that I must leave this!" He died in early March 1661, mourned by few, though Anne of Austria deeply attached to him was much grieved. His nephew and nieces did not bother to conceal their delight. "God be thanked he is gone" they exclaimed. "It is a remarkable thing," Hortense wrote, "that a man of that merit, after having laboured all his life to elevate and enrich his family, should have received from it, after his death, nothing but marks of aversion. But, if you knew with what severity he treated us in all things, you would be less surprised at it. Never had man manners so courteous in public and so harsh in his own house. All our tastes and inclinations were contrary to his, and to that must be added the incredible subjection in which we were held."[16]

Hortense and her husband were bequeathed the residue of her uncle's fortune, including the finer portion of the Palais Mazarin[17] and its wonderful pictures and statues. Olympe Comtesse de Soissons inherited 350,000 livres, and Mazarin had already purchased for her the lucrative and influential post of Superintendent of Queen Marie Thérèse's household, a convenient base for renewing her sexual liaison with Louis. Marianne Mancini, soon to be Duchesse de Bouillon, received 600,000 livres, but Marie was on the whole shabbily treated in comparison with her sisters, receiving a dowry of 100,000 livres per annum on her marriage to the Constable Colonna, 15,000 livres as expenses for her journey to Italy, and some valuable jewelry. Philippe, handsome, indolent and given to writing amorous verse, was bequeathed a part of the Palais Mazarin, the Palazzo Mazarini at the foot of the Quirinal in Rome, and 600,000 livres besides other property.

It is said that Marie just before her enforced journey to Italy to marry Prince Colonna called on Hortense and her husband in the Palais Mazarin. Disturbed by something strange in the wild-looking expression of the Duc Mazarin, she turned on the startled Hortense, exclaiming in colloquial Italian, "Crepa! Crepa! Tu sarai più infelice di mi."[18] Perhaps she had inherited her father's gifts as a seer.

CHAPTER II

The Duchess Mazarin and her Husband

Others besides the bridegroom's father expressed misgivings concerning the Duc Mazarin. The Maréchal de Clérembaut, for instance, remarked before Cardinal Mazarin's death, "his brain is disordered, his head is affected, he is a dead man."[1]

At first the couple lived fairly happily and luxuriously in the Palais Mazarin, surrounded by the exquisite statues, Titians, Raphaels and Giorgīones collected by the Cardinal. Among Mazarin's masterpieces were several pictures from Charles I of England's collection, bought through a German banker Jabach from the Commonwealth government when it disposed of the pictures. Armand Duc Mazarin having been born in 1632 was about thirteen years older than Hortense. Saint-Simon praises him too fulsomely in his Mémoires[2] but he is mostly writing from hearsay after talking to his contemporaries, having only met him once or twice in later life. "He was very good company," he wrote, "and well educated, magnificent in his tastes, his manners courtly . . . he was on intimate terms with the King who has never ceased to like him and to give him proofs of it, gracious affable and courtly in business matters . . ." His father had realized quite rightly that the Cardinal had erred in entrusting the responsibility of his vast wealth in his hands. His mind was neither stable nor strong enough to stand the strain.

By temperament the Duc Mazarin was obsessively jealous. In those. early days Hortense, thoughtless, frivolous and indiscreet, was far from blameless in giving her husband cause for such a sentiment. He resented Louis's too frequent visits to the Palais Mazarin, suspecting that the King was too much attracted to his wife. Hortense herself always denied that Louis ever showed excessive admiration for her. At twenty-three the King had been released from the shyness and inhibitions of adolescence, and that he owed to the beneficial influence of Marie Mancini, now the wife of the Prince Colonna. On Mazarin's death, Louis had lost no time in showing his ministers, much to their amazement, that he intended to govern himself. On assuming full powers, he devoted six to eight hours daily to work on state affairs. Marie Mancini's place had been taken during the enchanted summer of 1661 by Henriette d'Angleterre, Charles II's Minette, the charming wife of Louis's brother, the homosexual Monsieur Duc d'Orléans. So Fontainebleau was very gay with open-air balls, ballets and picnics amidst the beauty of sunlight and shadow in the forest glades of the Hermitage of Franchard. How resplendent it was to glide in his barge in the moonlight, listening to the strains of Lully, for the King always loved music.

If the Duc Mazarin had no real cause to be jealous of Louis, he had cause for resentment where another of her admirers was concerned, the Chevalier de Rohan. It induced him to introduce into her household a woman of good standing from Provence named Madame de Ruz, whose duty was to spy on her. After intercepting an amorous note written by Hortense to the Chevalier, he complained to the King. Louis lost no time in scolding Hortense. "What pains me most," he wrote the Bishop of Fréjus, "is the thought that a person who bears the name of so great a man should give everyone cause to laugh at her."[3] Her husband could not bear Hortense speaking to any of the servants in the Palais Mazarin. When she did so, he was immediately dismissed. He would not allow her to drive out in her own carriage, unless accompanied. His pathological jealousy of her family amounted almost to insanity and he particularly disliked her brother Philippe Duc de Nevers. A close bond undoubtedly existed between brother and sister, a highly charged, emotional relationship, and Mazarin later accused Hortense and Philippe of incest.

It is probable that the Duc suffered from a form of paranoia. He was too much in love with his wife ever to sleep alone. When at last she slept peacefully he would rouse her, avowing that he saw evil spirits around her bed. Nothing would satisfy him until his valets had searched the room. Her devoted friend Saint-Evrémond, a very prejudiced witness, later wrote of the Duc Mazarin:

"No sooner were the beautiful eyes of his companion closed, than this amiable husband, to whose black imagination the

26

devil was always present, awoke her to make her share his nocturnal visions. They lighted torches, they searched everywhere: but the only devil whom Madame de Mazarin found was the one with her in bed."[4]

Why did not Hortense rebel, protest at such treatment? It may well be that she thought her best course was to be patient, being very superstitious.

Saint-Simon relates in his Mémoires that the Duc Mazarin made himself ridiculous by demanding an interview with King Louis. His conscience, he said, had made him inform the King of the scandal which he was causing throughout France by his immoral relations with Louise de la Vallière,[5] his mistress. On another occasion he was bold enough to say that the Archangel Gabriel had appeared to him charging him to convey a similar message to the King. Louis not unreasonably told him that he had for a long time suspected that he was not quite right in the head. Now he was certain of it.

In her Mémoires Hortense complained that her husband, insisting that she was subject to too great temptations in Paris, forced her to accompany him to Maine, Nevers, Alsace and Brittany. He had a valid excuse for doing so since he held many important offices, such as the governorship of Alsace, Brittany and Vincennes. However, the Duc Mazarin had not the slightest consideration for her or regard for her health, forcing her to travel vast distances even when she was *enceinte*. Instead of providing luxurious accommodation he made her stay in rude inns or primitive cottages. No wife with spirit would submit patiently to such treatment. During the seven years they lived together Hortense gave birth to four children, three daughters and a son.

His eccentricity took many forms. One of his most marked qualities was his excessive prudishness. Yet Saint-Simon may have exaggerated the story that Armand wished to have his daughters' front teeth extracted fearing that they might become too attractive and fall into sinful ways.[6] Fearful that the women and girls on his estates might have immodest thoughts, he forbade them to milk cows.[7] When fire broke out at one of his country-houses, he was furious with his tenants for trying to extinguish it, saying it was sinful to oppose the will of God. Religious mania induced him to wander from one village to another preaching and exhorting like some itinerant friar. His servants found him quite impossible.

He was in the habit, for instance, of drawing lotteries for the various positions in his household. At times his cook would become his steward, while the man scrubbing the floors would find himself to his consternation the ducal secretary. It availed nothing for a footman to protest that he knew nothing whatever about cooking, for the Duc merely said: "You would not have been summoned to the post of cook without being provided with the necessary talents." God could decide best the tasks for which they were best fitted.

His crowning folly - one can call it insanity - was to order four hundred nude statues of immense value and artistic beauty to be destroyed. They must no longer be allowed to offend his own modesty or pollute the minds of others. This antique sculpture had been collected by Cardinal Mazarin from all over Europe. One night when Armand was at Vincennes he suddenly decided to leave for Paris. Arriving at the Palais Mazarin early in the morning he found Monsieur Tourolles, their custodian, still in bed. Despite his protests the Duc and a stone-mason spent the whole of the day armed with heavy hammers mutilating the treasures. On hearing of the affair King Louis sent his trusted Minister Jean-Baptiste Colbert, Cardinal Mazarin's former intendant, to the Palais Mazarin to try to stop the destruction. Despite his protests, he was powerless to prevent an illustrious nobleman such as the Duc Mazarin doing exactly what he liked with his own property. Who can divine the motives in the diseased mind of this man? Perhaps a brooding hatred of the Cardinal, suspecting that some of his wealth had been fraudulently acquired, mixed with resentment that Mazarin had for many years opposed his marriage to Hortense. Another of his foibles was a passion for litigation and Hortense was to suffer from this. Some of the suits concerned Mazarin property. If these cases were decided against him, he was wont to say that as he had no moral right to his enormous possessions, he welcomed the decision.

Mazarin was essentially monogamous and Hortense polyandrous by nature, so their marriage never had any chance of success. They should never have married, for he was the last person capable of handling Hortense. Yet its failure was by no means entirely his fault. Her amorous intrigues no doubt contributed to the mental disease within him. At times he would seem perfectly rational, at other times he would reveal the taint of madness in his diseased mind.

In desperation Hortense decided on flight. She had been bequeathed by her uncle some valuable jewels. If she were to see these, she would be able to live very comfortably apart from her husband. One night on going to fetch them she found that they had disappeared. When she taxed her husband with the theft, he told her with an unpleasant leer on his face: "You are of so liberal a nature that I fear you may give some away." "I wish your liberality had been as regular as mine" exclaimed Hortense. Then she used a woman's weapon. "I'll not come to bed until I have them." Mazarin refused to part with her jewelry.

She sought refuge with her younger sister Marianne, now the Duchesse de Bouillon. She was not at first very sympathetic at her plight. "You are well enough served," she told her sister, "since you have suffered so much already without saying a word." Marianne was very pretty like all the Mancini sisters, with an audacious little retroussé nose. A subtle enigmatic smile lit up her dainty little face. During his lifetime Cardinal Mazarin had not considered the Duc de Bouillon a sufficiently good parti, though a nephew of the great Turenne, but she had married him in 1662 after her uncle's death. She was as devoted to literature, being the patroness of La Fontaine the poet and other renowned writers, as her husband was to soldiering. While the Duc de Bouillon was fighting against the Turks in Hungary, Marianne became intimate with La Fontaine, who owed much to her inspiration and encouragement. The poet was to call her later "The mother of all the loves and queen of all the graces." However, she showed ill-judgment in supporting a protégé of her own, a poet called Pradon and trying to harm the career of the great Racine.

Hortense lived apart from her husband for about two months, returned to him temporarily and fled from him again after making terrible scenes. She now refused to accompany the Duc when he travelled to Alsace, where he was governor, though agreeing to enter a convent, the Abbaye de Chelles, during his absence.

There much to her husband's anger she got on very well with the Abbess of Chelles, who was the Duc's own aunt. A real friendship grew between them. When Mazarin returned from Alsace he succeeded in persuading King Louis, only partly aware of how the marriage had deteriorated, that she should be transferred to the far stricter nunnery of the Filles de St. Marie at the Bastille. While at Chelles she had already instituted an action for separation of goods against her husband in the Court of Requests. Although far more strictly treated at the Filles de St. Marie Convent, Hortense formed a delightful new friendship with Sidonie de Leconcourt Marquise de Courcelles. This lovely girl had been incarcerated here by her husband, a worthless and avaricious man, who had married her for her fortune. He made a sordid compact with the Marquis de Louvois, one of King Louis's chief ministers, who was madly in love with her. He would get her money while she became Louvois's mistress. Although she never cared for the latter, her passionate love affair with the Marquis de Villeroi gave her unpleasant husband sufficient excuse to put her in a convent.

Hortense and Sidonie, both high-spirited and sparkling with a zest for life, and both excellent company, indulged in all sorts of pranks in the nunnery. Hortense relates:

> "I had the complacency to join with her in some pleasantries which she played upon the nuns. A hundred absurd tales about this were told the King, that we put ink in the holy-water basin to blacken the faces of the nuns, that we careered through the dormitories accompanied by a pack of dogs making hunting noises . . ."

All these stories, Hortense wrote, were grossly exaggerated . . .

> "It is true that we filled a large coffer which stood in our dormitory with water, and the boards of the floor being very loosely joined together, it had leaked through the backs and flooded the beds of the nuns in the floor below."[8]

Her husband now obtained an order from the Archbishop of Paris to permit him to enter the Convent to take Hortense away.

Accompanied by an escort of sixty guards, he appeared before the Abbey determined to seize his wife, but Hortense defiantly stood before a grill, having been handed the keys by the Abbess, and refused to admit him. Much to his fury the Duc Mazarin was compelled to return to Paris empty-handed. On the following day, seeing a large body of horse approaching the abbey, Hortense fearing that it was her husband with reinforcements, hid herself in the chimney of her room, where she was nearly suffocated by the soot. To her enormous relief, however, she found that it was a party of relations and friends, including Marianne and her husband, the Duc de Bouillon, together with the Comte de Soissons, who had come to her rescue.

Meanwhile, the Court of Requests decided the suit for separation of goods in Hortense's favour, but Mazarin appealed to the great Chamber of Justice, who were expected to reverse the decision of the lower Court. When Louis XIV intervened in their quarrels, a temporary accommodation was reached with his agreement, whereby Hortense and the Duc were to occupy separate apartments in the Palais Mazarin. She was to be allowed the right to choose her own household, but Monsieur Colbert, the King's chief minister, would select her equerry. Perhaps Louis considered, quite rightly, that Hortense was not to be trusted where men were concerned. She was no longer obliged to accompany her husband on his journeys. Such an accommodation had little chance of success, and in any case neither party had the slightest intention to abide by it. So it was terminated and Louis, on Hortense's insistence, promised her that he would never intervene in her matrimonial affairs again.

Now determined to be free of her husband and fearing that the great Chamber of Justice would order her to resume cohabitation with the Duc Mazarin, Hortense came to the desperate decision to flee from him and leave France. He had certainly given her enough provocation. Surely the most fateful decision of her life.

CHAPTER III

Her Flight

Two men planned her flight; her own brother Philippe Duc de Nevers and the Chevalier de Rohan, who had earlier been suspected of a love intrigue with Hortense. However, in her Mémoires she insists that their relations were innocent. Whatever the truth it was unwise and indiscreet of her to employ him in her adventures. It was Wednesday June 13th 1668[1] when Hortense, accompanied by her faithful maid Nanon, a servant of her brother's named Narcissus and Courbeville, a gentleman in the household of the Chevalier de Rohan, escaped from Paris. According to her own account, if it can be relied on, the Chevalier did not accompany her beyond the gates of Paris. In the hurry of departure Hortense discovered when she reached the Porte St. Antoine that she had forgotten her casket of jewels, and these had hastily to be sent for from the Palais Mazarin.

At first the party travelled rather slowly in a calèche, Hortense and Nanon dressed in breeches in male attire, thinking that they would better escape detection by this guise. For Hortense life was everything.

Despite the danger, she was already beginning to enjoy herself, laughingly telling her maid how absurd she looked in her breeches. At Bar in Lorraine, where they arrived on a Friday, Hortense exchanged her calèche to travel on horseback, and so reached Nancy without being discovered.

Meanwhile, Duc Mazarin did not discover her flight until the middle of the night (June 13th), for her attendants pretended she was ill and confined to her apartments. Greatly agitated, he hurried to the Louvre where he arrived about 3 a.m. insisting on waking the King to inform him, who was by no means pleased. "Did not the Angel Gabriel warn you of this?" he asked with a slightly ironic smile. Contrary to popular belief Louis possessed a wry sense of humour. "Pray give orders for her to be pursued and for the local governors to have her arrested," implored the angry Mazarin. The King reminded him that he had given his solemn word that he would henceforward refrain from interfering in her affairs. In any case it was probable that she was already out of France, so that orders to stop her would be absolutely useless. Colbert, however, who never cared for the Mancinis, was more sympathetic, suggesting that the Duc should send some sort of emissary after her to try to induce her to return. Mazarin decided to send one of the Lieutenants of the Ordnance named La Louvière for that purpose.

Henriette d'Angleterre Duchesse d'Orléans was in the habit of writing her brother what transpired at the French Court. When she informed him of Hortense's flight - he had once been her suitor - Charles was much intrigued, writing his sister: "The sudden retreate of Madame Mazarin is as extraordinaire an action as I have heard," he told Madam (as she was called by her contemporaries). "She has exceeded My Lady Shrewsbery (Mistress of the Duke of Buckingham) in point of discretion by robbing her husband (this is untrue, but Charles had heard some unreliable rumour). I see wives do not love devoute husbands which reason this woman had besides many more as I heare to be rid of her husband upon any tearmes, and so I wish her a good journey."[2] He could not resist adding in his humourous way: "I am sorry to find that cucolds in France grow so troublesome, they have been inconvenient in all countries this last yeare."

Owing to her beauty and charm Hortense always found it easy to get people of influence and authority to help her. In Nancy the gallant Duke of Lorraine was only too ready to provide a Lieutenant and twenty guards to conduct her safely into Switzerland. She was at heart a child, irresponsible, carefree, high-spirited and accustomed to be spoilt. According to her account in her Mémoires she was indulging in horseplay with her maid Nanon when she hurt her knee so badly that she was compelled to continue her journey by litter as far as Neuchâtel. She tells us that for some weeks she feared that gangrene would set in. Where Courbeville acquired his medical skill is not known, but Hortense was grateful to him for his care and solicitude in treating her leg. She took a violent fancy to him and he was much enamoured of her.

She soon became his mistress. It was natural enough in the circumstances for Nanon and Narcissus to resent their mistress's marked attentions to Courbeville since she was closeted with him for several hours alone.

Her husband's envoy La Louvière arrived as she was crossing the Italian border, bearing irate messages accusing her of being de Rohan's mistress (she was clearly Courbeville's mistress). He accused her of the highest infamy and lewdness with Philippe, her brother, even of incest, having discovered some alleged passionate love poems addressed to her. Nevers wrote that his sister was more beautiful than Lucrece, but also more chaste than Venus, so there was almost certainly little substance in such a grave charge. The Duc Mazarin, however, took legal action against his brother-in-law, but the judges decided against him.

When Hortense had reached the neighbourhood of Milan, her sister Marie and her husband the Prince Colonna, met her at a country house belonging to the Colonnas and escorted her to Milan. Instead of showing some gratitude to Marie for her kindness, Hortense was tactless enough to laugh without restraint at the outmoded fashions worn by her and the other Italian ladies. Marie always hypersensitive was extremely hurt.

Marie's first meeting with Lorenzo Colonna in Italy can hardly be described a success. By way of a practical joke Prince Colonna made one of his closest friends, the Marques Spinola de Los Balbases (an Italian by birth) greet her first and pretend to be her husband. Balbases was rather older than Colonna and was by no means attractive, while Marie's husband had many handsome features. Marie tactlessly said to one of her attendants in French "If this were the husband intended for her, she would decline to have him. Let him seek a wife elsewhere."[3] Unfortunately she incurred the enmity of the Marques de Los Balbases, who never forgot the insult. By marrying Colonna's sister he became his brother-in-law. Marie was relieved when Colonna was pointed out as her real husband.

For the first five years of her marriage, Marie lived happily enough with her husband, though at first suffering from ill-health and a form of brain-fever owing to her experiences in France and the rigours of the journey to Italy. Sometimes she felt desperately

homesick for Louis and the French Court. Not only was Lorenzo
Onofrio Prince Colonna High Constable of Naples at first a most
considerate husband, but he was much in love with Marie, showing
her every indulgence and allowing her to live à la Française, the
freedom to receive whoever and wherever she wanted. This was
much criticized by the Roman nobility accustomed as they were
to keep very close surveillance over their wives. Colonna on his
part, according to the Mémoires of the Duchesse Mazarin, believing "that the love of Kings could not be innocent, was so delighted
to find the contrary in the person of my sister, that he made no
account of not being the first who had gained her heart." More-
over she gave her husband three sons, Filippo Principe di Palliano,
Marco Antonio and Carlo.

Then for no apparent reason she told her husband that she
did not intend to sleep with him any more. Possibly because an
astrologer - and Marie was clearly keenly interested in the subject
like her mother and father - had warned her that the birth of a
fourth child would cause her own death. Far more likely that
Marie had discovered that Colonna was a far from faithful husband
and that he had a little girl Maria by another woman. How dare he
call her Maria? Marie stormed at Lorenzo, refusing to share him
with his mistress, and to go to bed with him. Very soon the gossip
mongers of Rome and the news-sheets reported the *separazione di
letto* of Prince and Princess Colonna. They went to Venice, Marie's
favourite Italian city, where she enjoyed herself enormously at the
Carnival (1665), but her husband was infatuated with the lovely
Marchesa Paleotto whom he installed for a time in vacant apartments in the Palazzo Colonna. Such was the uneasy state of affairs
when Marie and the Constable left for Milan to meet her sister
Hortense.

Unable to resist her sister's charm, Marie was delighted to see
her, but Hortense showed no desire to seek their company, giving
out that she had recently sustained a fall from a horse and needed
complete rest and seclusion. They soon discovered that her real
reason for her peculiar behaviour was that she wanted to be alone
with her lover Courbeville. When Philippe Duc de Nevers arrived in
Milan to see Hortense, Nanon and Narcissus seized the opportunity to tell Philippe that Courbeville had spoken insolently about

him. In her Mémoires, Marie wrote that Hortense was giving her lover un peu trop d'ailes, treating him as an equal. Thoroughly enraged, Philippe threatened to throw Courbeville out of the window if he did not immediately return to France. He was furious that Hortense called Courbeville "Monsieur le Chevalier", although he had no right to that title.

The Colonnas took Philippe's part, but she refused to part with Courbeville and family relations became more and more strained. Eventually she agreed to dismiss her lover, but Courbeville desperately in love with Hortense, knelt before her, imploring her to let him stay. "I cannot return to my master, the Chevalier de Rohan," he said, "without carrying my head to the scaffold. I shall be utterly ruined if you discharge me."[4] Moved by his words, Hortense gave way, allowing him to stay.

When they returned to Rome, Marie had a row with Courbeville in the Palazzo Colonna. To get rid of him she cried: "Go! You will get your deserts in the courtyard." "Not unless the Duchess (Mazarin) decrees it," said her lover. "I will be commanded by none but her." However, Hortense in a fit of temper left her sister's Palazzo for the house of her uncle Cardinal Mancini. She was with child by Courbeville, but she never mentions her illegitimate offspring in her Mémoires. Fearing for his safety, Courbeville left hurriedly for Civita Vecchia where he tried to board a ship for France, but Prince Colonna had him arrested and imprisoned for a time in a fortress. Grateful no doubt for past services, Hortense obtained his release through the intercession of Francesco Rospigliosi, the Pope's nephew.

Hortense was very upset when she heard that her husband had succeeded in obtaining an order from the Parliament in Paris, allowing him to have her arrested wherever she might be. He pestered the Pope incessantly. Hortense must be compelled to enter a convent. She soon moved to the house of her aunt Madame Martinozzi, mother of the Duchess of Modena, where she amused herself playing the guitar. Then of her own accord she returned to the Convent of Campo-Marzo, where she did pretty well what she liked, until Marie, with whom she had been reconciled, bore her off to the Palazzo Colonna, much to the anger of the nuns. According to Hortense's account "My poor old aunt (the Abbess) took the matter so much to heart that she died a few days later of the guilt my escape had occasioned her." Hortense might have stayed with Queen Christina of Sweden, now in exile in Rome, but hearing that she was expecting a baby the Queen cancelled the invitation.

Hortense and Marie lived in magnificent apartments in the Palazzo Colonna. In the salons fountains constantly played and the courtyards were cool, while outside the Roman heat of summer beat down on the noisy streets. When Marie was first pregnant her husband had ordered a resplendent bed to be made for her consisting of a golden shell held together by four sea-horses ridden by mermaids in an azure sea.

The spring of 1670 was very gay in Rome, for there were continual fêtes to celebrate the election of Cardinal Rospigliosi as Pope Clement X. Hortense, who only lived for pleasure at this period, enjoyed herself enormously. How beautiful the Piazza Navonna seemed with torch-bearers lighting up the scene, transformed for the fiesta into a lake where boats plied to and fro and musicians played soft music.

Surrounded by a host of admirers and would-be lovers, Hortense soon forgot Courbeville. Among her most favoured suitors was a young and very handsome Norman gentleman named Jacques de Belboeuf, son of a Counsellor of the Parliament of Normandy, who was completing his education in Rome. For a time they became lovers, and de Belboeuf could not refrain from telling his mother that Hortense had given him her portrait, "I beg you to make what use of it you think fit, but it is most important not to let it out of your keeping and do no allow people to finger it."[5]

Jealousy was rife among Hortense's lovers. It fell to the Prince Colonna himself passionate and quarrelsome to have to separate an Italian nobleman to whom she had also given her portrait from a less favoured rival, who had challenged him to a duel. Hortense might be one of the most beautiful and desirable women of her time, but it is probable that she took little pleasure in seeing her admirers fighting for her affections. In her amiable way she found it a nuisance.

Always extravagant she had by now spent almost all her money, so that she was obliged even to pawn her jewels. She

37

borrowed money from a friend of her brother Philippe, but the Marquese del Grillo later made it clear that he expected in return she would grant him her favours. However, he did not appeal to Hortense. She now decided to return temporarily to France in a desperate attempt to induce her husband to give her a pension.

It so happened that her brother the Duc de Nevers, who had returned to Rome where he lived in his palace, was about to start for France to marry the lovely Diane de Thianges, niece of Louis XIV's reigning mistress Madame de Montespan. Now reconciled to Philippe, she decided impulsively to accompany him on his journey. Their travels took several months. On reaching Nevers Hortense was aghast to learn that her husband Armand had sent Polastron, Captain of the guard, with a band of soldiers, having instructed him to arrest her by order of Parliament. Fortunately the people of Nevers took her part. It soon became apparent that King Louis intended to impose his own authority. He sent an escort of his guards, who conducted her to the Abbaye de Lys, where she was to remain three months.

In her Mémoires Hortense declared that Louis treated her very kindly, receiving her in the apartments of Madame de Montespan in Paris and putting two alternatives to her. Either she could return to her husband with whom she would not be expected to resume marital relations or, if she felt absolutely unable to do this, she could return to Italy where he would undertake that a pension of 24,000 livres per annum was settled on her. He urged her to return to her husband, encouraged by Madame de Montespan and Madame Colbert, the wife of Louis's minister. The Marquise Françoise-Athénais de Montespan, beautiful and avaricious as she undoubtedly was, could hardly give Hortense disinterested advice, for she feared such a seductive woman as a possible rival to her own supremacy at Court. Despite their strong persuasion, Hortense after expressing suitable expressions of gratitude to the King, decided in favour of returning to Rome. After inheriting many millions she considered 24,000 livres a niggardly pension. The Duc de Lauzun told her that she would undoubtedly spend it "at the first inn she stopped in," and the courtiers had not the slightest confidence when Hortense assured them: "By this time I know how to husband my money."

Armand Mazarin now protested in the strongest terms to King Louis that his wife was leaving him without his consent. He took umbrage particularly when she was provided with funds for a journey for which he had not given his permission. It reflected on his honour. Louis merely told him that Hortense seemed to have decided not to return to him. To every attempt to persuade her otherwise she would respond with the battle-cry of the Fronde: "Point de Mazarin! Point de Mazarin!"[6]

So the Duchesse Mazarin returned to Rome, breaking her journey at Turin where Charles-Emmanuel Duke of Savoy, her former suitor at Lyon, gave her such a warm reception that she immediately resolved that if it was necessary to seek refuge again she would return to his territories.

Meanwhile the strained relations between Marie and Lorenzo Colonna had worsened. It was no secret, for all Rome discussed it. News-letters such as the Gazette de Leyden relate:

"The bad feeling which exists between them is known to every one. It is believed that His Excellency the Marquis d'Astorges, Viceroy of Naples, will discuss the matter previous to his departure for Naples and endeavour to bring about a reconciliation."

But the couple remained estranged. The Prince Colonna, a man of violent temper, with a reputation for assassinating his enemies if they provoked him, was only partly to blame for the break-up of his marriage. Marie must share some of the blame. Restless and capricious by temperament, she had been given too much license in the early days of their marriage when the Constable was genuninely in love with his wife. She indulged in several love affairs or flirtations whilst living with Lorenzo Colonna, though these were hardly of a serious nature.

She was temporarily the mistress of Ernst August, Duke of Brunswick-Luneburg Elector of Hanover[7] when he came to Italy with his wife Sophie. This German prince with a roving eye much admired Hortense, too, and gave both sisters presents of jewellery. While Sophie was awaiting Ernst August in Venice, he stayed at Madam Colonna's villa in the country. The Electress of Hanover later wrote rather tartly:

> "But Madam Colonna is mistaken when she prints in her Mémoires that he left for his visit to her when I arrived in Rome. Her wit may be better than mine, but her memory is worse. He only went after I had gone."[8]

Her description of Marie after one of her accouchements "sitting up in bed, wearing an odd-looking blue and silver Neapolitan jacket fastened down the front with flame-coloured ribbons" is not at all flattering. In Rome Marie acted as the Electress of Hanover's guide, taking her to see Bernini's masterpiece St. Peters and other churches. Hortense also relates in her Mémoires that the Constable Colonna, a passionate Italian, resented his wife's flirtations during the Venice Carnival and on one occasion had insisted on her leaving the city. Perhaps Marie indulged in these little affairs as a form of revenge for Lorenzo Colonna's love affairs with the Marchese Paleotto and the Princess Chigi, one of the great ladies of Rome.

For some time Marie and Hortense were on very friendly terms with the Chevalier de Lorraine, who together with his brother, the Comte de Marsan, had been living in Rome. Philippe de Lorraine was an exile, having been banished from France owing to Madame's (the Duchesse d'Orléan's) influence with her brother-in-law King Louis, unable to endure any longer Lorraine's insolence and his homosexual relations with her husband Monsieur. She had insisted on his banishment. Then at the end of June 1670 Madame (Charles the Second's Minette) died suddenly and tragically after returning to France from her celebrated mission to Dover. Some of her contemporaries were convinced she had been poisoned.[9] Cold-shouldered as he was for the most part in Rome, Lorraine was grateful to Marie and Hortense for giving him and his brother such a warm reception. They had known the Mancini sisters well in France in the early days. Marie, too, had always remained on very friendly terms with Monsieur, a faithful friend, sending him presents from Italy, such as perfumes and gloves, by a trusy messenger. In return Monsieur sent her an elegant hunting outfit with one thousand pistoles.

40

While Hortense favoured the Comte de Marsan, Marie indulged in a close friendship - some said a love affair - with the Chevalier de Lorraine, a godson of Anne of Austria (she had died in 1666) and the late Cardinal Mazarin. Lorraine had little to recommend him except a very handsome face 'fait comme on peint les anges' as the Abbé de Choissy - a contemporary - described him. Marie certainly liked the Chevalier, taking pleasure in his conversation, for he would have all the latest news of the French Court and of Louis himself. Lorenzo Colonna was very jealous of Lorraine's relations with his wife, though the affair as such was hardly serious. Most of all he not unnaturally disapproved of Lorraine painting Marie's portrait in a diaphanous robe, which she sometimes wore when bathing in the Tiber. It was indiscreet of her, possibly leading to misunderstanding. Pierre Mignard's portrait of Marie in the Berlin gallery depicts her as a woman of sparkling vivacity and considerable beauty.

Colonna, who had once loved her, was by this time tired of Marie. One night she lay in terrible pain suffering from a colic, but according to her Mémoires the Constable Colonna did not seem to mind, as he listened to her complaints. At that period the crime of poisoning was very prevalent in Italy. Whether Marie had real justification for suspecting that her husband was attempting to poison her is difficult to determine. If Colonna were to commit a crime, it is more likely that it would be one of violence. Now as Marie was recuperating from her illness, her devoted Moorish maid Moréna, who had accompanied her from France and hated the Constable, brought her a letter addressed to him. Marie's nature essentially frank and open, made her loath to open it, but Moréna implored her mistress to do so, telling her rather naively that she must not lose any opportunity of discovering whether her husband wanted her to die. The mysterious letter seemed to confirm her suspicions, for the correspondent warned the Prince that his wife was suffering from an incurable malady. There was mention of a more advantageous marriage intended by Colonna.

Fearing for her life, Marie immediately confided her suspicions to the Chevalier de Lorraine. They both agreed to write to Monsieur informing him of the desperate state of affairs and imploring him to lay the two letters before the King. On January 22nd 1672 Louis wrote to the Bishop of Laon (Cardinal d'Estrées French Ambassador in Rome) informing him that he had decided to recall the Chevalier de Lorraine and the Comte de Marsan from their exile.[10] At his interview with King Louis during March, Lorraine warned His Majesty as strongly as possible that Marie was in great danger, convinced as he was that her recent illness had not been owing to natural causes. It was vital to protect her from any further attempts upon her life by her husband. Alarmed for the safety of the woman he had once loved, Louis gave assurances to Marie, promising her his protection and a passport immediately she landed in France. She was to inform him of the port where she intended to disembark.

Marie's disillusion, her inevitable restlessness and disenchantment with her marriage does not make her an altogether reliable witness regarding her husband's alleged guilt. A fixed obsession possessed her mind to return to France. Once again a desperate longing to see Louis motivated her actions. Sometimes she seemed to hear his ardent voice bidding his tender adieux, vowing that he would give her proofs of his esteem and attachment wherever she might be. In her heart she could not believe that the King would not give her a cordial welcome when she returned to France. Of course she knew about his mistresses, La Vallière, the shy flower, who had given him children, and Madame de Montespan, with whom he was infatuated. Could Louis have so much changed? Remembering the past, she over-estimated her power over her former lover. If she could not be his Queen, her fatal pride had forbidden her to be his mistress. In her arrogance as the wife of a great Italian noble she even thought that the Pope, Alexander VII of the Chigi family, should call on her, but she had to submit to being escorted by Princess Chigi to pay homage to His Holiness in the Vatican.

Marie now confided to Hortense that she had decided on the desperate course of fleeing from her husband. Mindful of her own experiences when fleeing from Mazarin, Hortense used every conceivable argument in her attempt to dissuade her sister from such a reckless action, but Marie had made up her mind. She tried to justify her decision:

"The violent conduct of the Constable, joined to the aversion I entertained for Italian customs, and for the manner of life at Rome"

Marie relates in her Mémoires,

"where dissimulation and hatred between families are more in vogue than at other Courts, hastened my desire to return to France."

Hortense suspected that these reasons were mostly subterfuges. What her sister really wanted was to regain her hold over Louis. For her part she had no desire to remain in Italy without Marie, thinking that she might be able to lessen the dangers she would be obliged to incur by sharing them with her.[11] Hortense intended to make for Savoy, where she would have a powerful protector in the Duke of Savoy. While she remained on French soil, the persecution by her husband presented a hideous menace.

The sisters laid their plans very carefully. They were aware that towards the end of May 1672 Prince Colonna intended a visit to one of his stud farms about twelve miles from Rome. Meanwhile one of Hortense's servants, her groom of the Chamber, whose name was Pelletier, a resourceful and loyal man, had been entrusted with a secret mission to Naples to arrange with the Captain of a boat that they should be transported to France. Financial terms were naturally discussed. It was agreed that the adventuresses should embark from Civita Vecchia.

CHAPTER IV

More Adventures

It was May 29th, a fateful day in the lives of both sisters. Hortense, attended by Pelletier, her waiting-woman Nanon and a footman, awaited Marie at the Palazzo Mancini. When Marie arrived, accompanied by the faithful Moréna, they cried to their coachman 'To Frascati' to deceive a cluster of inquisitive bystanders before the palazzo, but they soon ordered him to drive to Civita Vecchia. Under their own clothes the two women and their servants were dressed in male outfit, having very little baggage. Marie took with her the much cherished pearl necklace given her by King Louis, but she thoughtfully left behind her to be divided among her children the remainder of her jewels possessed by her since her marriage.

Marie's account of their adventures is more detailed and dramatic than Hortense's. They reached the outskirts of Civita Vecchia only to find the gates of the town were shut, so they went into a little wood where they slept so soundly that "Nanon, my sister's maid, and Moréna who was with me and mounted guard over us, were astonished to the last degree to see us sleeping so tranquilly . . ." Meanwhile Marie's footman, who had been sent to find the boat, got drunk in an inn and failed to return. The trustworthy Pelletier, aided by a postillion called La Roche, was more fortunate in his quest. La Roche returned on horseback to say that he had found the felucca originally chartered. When she heard the sound of a galloping horse, Hortense, who possessed more physical courage and resilience than her sister, stood with a loaded pistol in each hand in case of necessity. Marie tells of the hardships endured by both sisters, Hortense apparently tireless, while Marie almost fainted from weariness and from the heat of the Italian sun. It was necessary for them to trudge "through a flat country, in which we saw a number of vipers gliding about". There were five miles to cover before reaching the sea and the felucca, which they hoped

44

would take them into safety. "The indefatigable Madame Mazarin constituted herself our advance guard" related Marie, "and contrived to walk so fast that, to keep up with her, I was forced to rest from time to time." "Hunger, thirst, weariness and the heat had deprived me of strength to such a degree that I was compelled to ask a man, who was engaged in ploughing, to carry me some hundred paces towards the sea." Then Hortense and Marie saw two vessels, the one originally hired by Pelletier, traced by La Roche, and the other newly chartered by Pelletier.

Since he had a high opinion of the honesty of the Master of the first vessel, they decided to sail in her, but not before the Master and the crew of the second vessel had turned very nasty, "threatening to prevent us putting out to sea". So they were forced to give them money to free them from that difficulty. When Pelletier with a very troubled expression on his face pretended by way of pleasantry that they were pursued, Hortense was very angry. When she heard it was untrue she sharply rebuked him.

Scarcely out at sea, the Master of the first vessel demanded more money than the original amount agreed between Pelletier and himself. He got very angry, but Marie and Hortense were hardly in a position to dispute the matter because the man threatened to throw them overboard or cast them ashore on a deserted island unless they submitted to his demands. He stressed the dangers he was running in taking them to France. At this juncture Marie thought it prudent to add one hundred pistoles to the sum previously agreed to, promising the Captain further recompense when they arrived safely at their destination. The crew supposed that the ladies were fugitives from justice, Hortense being much amused when asked whether she had murdered the Pope. During the voyage the Captain sighted what he thought was a ship containing Turkish pirates, so rather than risk falling into their hands, he landed on the coast of Tuscany for the night. Continuing their voyage in very calm weather they arrived at Monaco where Marie tells us the sea became very rough under the influence of a very high wind. Both sisters suffered from sea-sickness, but Hortense worse than Marie. Having obtained false certificates of health, they sailed for the port of Ciotat in Provence, a voyage taking nine days undertaken in excruciating discomfort.

At Marseilles they felt heartened when handed passports, and a letter to Marie from King Louis. There was a further letter from the Foreign Minister Simon Arnauld Pomponne, to the Comte de Grignan, the King's Lieutenant in Provence, and Madame de Sévigné's son-in-law, asking him to receive the Princess of Colonna at Aix and to give her every assistance. His wife Madame de Grignan, most thoughtfully provided the sisters with clean linen.

Meanwhile Prince Colonna, having returned from the stud and having discovered Marie's flight and that of the Duchesse Mazarin, made frantic attempts to ascertain their whereabouts. As a great nobleman the Constable Colonna feared ridicule, but he was more apprehensive that a false account would be given King Louis concerning his treatment of Marie. He therefore wrote the King of France (June 21st 1672) requesting his powerful protection and referring to some charges brought against him as "imaginary pretexts".[1] Colonna, hearing that Marie and her sister were in Aix, sent an emissary named Meneghini there, who succeeded in tracing Marie and Hortense. They were lodging in an inn in Aix. Seeing that they were exhausted with fatigue, the envoy courteously implored Marie in the name of the Constable Colonna to return to Rome. Marie, however, was adamant in refusing his plea. All sorts of rumours were rampant that Hortense and Marie's real purpose was to rejoin their lovers Lorraine and Marsan.

Madame de Grignan immediately informed her mother, Madame de Sévigné, of the adventures of the Duchesse Mazarin and of Madame de Colonna. It created a terrific sensation in Paris and indeed throughout Europe. That most gifted and entertaining writer of letters informed her daughter:

> "In the midst of our afflictions, the description you have given me of Madame Colonna and her sister is something divine; it inspires an air of joy and gaiety under the most melancholy circumstances."

Always intrigued by the antics and the follies of the Mancinis, she told her daughter that even their own sisters, Olympe and Marianne, indulging in a fit of morality were most active in declaring that they ought to be imprisoned, condemning their "extravagant folly".[2] What probably annoyed Olympe and Marianne was the freedom their sisters were claiming as their right to do whatever they liked with their lives. Madame de Scudery even suggested that corporal punishment was the only thing to do them good.

Hortense and Marie moved restlessly around Southern France, travelling from Mirabeau to Montpellier and thence to Monfrein. There Hortense heard that her husband on learning of her presence in France, had sent Polastron, Captain of his Guards, armed with the Parliament's order to arrest her. Much agitated, she concealed herself among the fish-ponds in the garden of the house where she was staying. When Polastron arrived he was told by the resourceful Marie that Hortense had already departed. Believing her story, Polastron left on a false scent in hot pursuit. Convinced that it was too dangerous for her to remain in France, Hortense travelled by water down the Rhone to Arles, eventually arriving in Turin, where she eagerly put herself under the protection of Charles-Emmanuel of Savoy.

Meanwhile the Prince Colonna, only too aware of the scandal Marie's flight was creating in Rome, made frantic appeals to King Louis, to the Pope and to her brother Philippe Duc de Nevers to use their influence to make her return to him. Deeply resentful, he threatened to confine her in one of his country houses or in a convent if she returned to him. Marie only thought of getting to Paris, where she might obtain an interview with her former royal lover. For that purpose she sent Pelletier to Holland, where King Louis was campaigning during the early summer, to beg him to grant his permission for her to come to Paris.

Unfortunately the roads were infested with brigands. Pelletier during his journey was attacked by Italian robbers, leaving him seriously wounded by the road-side.[3] Pelletier never reached Holland.

When Marie arrived in Grenoble she received a letter from Louis's Queen Marie Thérèse ordering her firmly, but courteously, "not to proceed beyond the place where Her Majesty's letter might find her". Louis's Spanish-born Queen had been constituted regent during the King's absence from his kingdom. Naturally enough, being very jealous by nature and mindful of her husband's former passion for Marie Mancini, she was opposed to the King

47

reviving his friendship with the Princess Colonna. Marie's brother Philippe, when he arrived in Grenoble, implored his sister to return to her husband, warning her that the influence of Louis's mistress, Madame de Montespan, and the enmity of the Queen, would combine to keep the King and Marie apart.

Philippe de Nevers was under pressure not only from his brother-in-law, but from the Pope and from his connection with Madame de Montespan through his marriage with her niece Diane de Thianges. He was right in one respect. Knowing Louis intimately as he did, he considered that the egotistical King would not hesitate to sacrifice Marie. She, however, was too determined and capricious to be deterred by his advice and started on the treacherous road for Paris.

Charles-Emmanuel Duke of Savoy welcomed Hortense eagerly to the Court of Savoy, and with his usual generosity offered to place the Château of Chambéry at her disposal. His court was one of the most brilliant in Europe. His wife Marie-Jeanne de Savoie-Nemours, having been born in 1646, was about ten years younger than her husband, and passionately attached to him, despite his numerous infidelities. From the first she resented Charles-Emmanuel's marked attentions to Hortense Mazarin. He possessed immense power in his kingdom, ruling it like a petty sovereign. While the aristocracy lived in splendour, surrounded by works of art, the country people were much impoverished, so that travellers were obliged to take refuge in primitive, filthy inns. Such was the provincial life of the later seventeenth century in the kingdom of Savoy, providing a complete contrast between the primitive and the idyllic. Charles-Emmanuel treated Hortense like a spoilt, capricious child, indulging her every whim, providing grooms and carriages when she went on journeys and thoughtfully supplying for her needs game, fruit and wine. When her sisters Olympe and Marianne in France heard that Hortense was living a life of ease and luxury at the expense of the Duke of Savoy, they could not conceal their fury.

Hortense was about to leave for the Château of Chambéry when she received a message from Marie asking her sister to join her at Grenoble. To make the journey as agreeable as possible, Charles-Emmanuel ordered his officers to receive her with every honour and to give her all possible assistance. The Governor of Montmeillan, a small town near Chambéry, reported to his master:

> "The Duchesse de Mazarin arrived here on Saturday evening towards nine o'clock . . . The next day I went down to the town to see her and to ask her to come and dine at the Château. She replied that she was in a hurry to proceed towards Grenoble to see her sister."

The poor man must have been heartily glad to get rid of her, for after lending her his light carriage and providing her with flasks of Piedmont wine and ice, and four baskets of game:

> "She had it all put into my carriage and having quaffed a goblet, she herself got in. She overturned three or four times; she had smashed my carriage, and very nearly killed one of my horses. At times she rode on the courser my groom was riding, at other times she preferred one of the carriage-horses."

At Grenoble Marie was deeply mortified to hear that Louis not only forbade her to come to Paris, but had refused to grant her an audience. How bitterly she reflected that thirteen years ago she had been treated at Louis's Court like a Queen. A visionary by temperament, she dreamt of the time when she used to read French and Italian poetry to the lovesick Louis, or again at seventeen reading Corneille aloud to the admiring courtiers in Queen Anne of Austria's circle.

Only one thought possessed her: to reach Paris and to obtain an interview with the King. She travelled partly by coach, urging her coachman to drive ever more speedily, causing the coach to overturn. When the ruts in the roads were too bad, she took to the water, travelling by boat. At last she arrived, almost penniless at Fontainebleau.

Dante, that superb Italian poet, has written that 'Nessun maggior dolor che ricordarsi del tempo felice nella miseria'. (No greater grief than to recall a happy time in wretchedness. Canto V *The Inferno*.) It was as if Marie wanted to taste the bitter last dregs of deprivation and adversity. Instead of accepting the invitation of the Duke of Modena (a cousin of the Mancinis) to stay at his palazzo, she chose instead a wretched auberge.

The Duc de Léqui, First Gentleman of the Bedchamber to Louis XIV, found her in a mean room together with her maid Moréna, her baggage, her guitar hung on the wall, and her little dog curled on the eiderdown. After commiserating with her plight - Marie was too proud to accept his sympathy - he broke the cruel news to her that Louis did not wish her to enter Paris or to speak to her, because he had promised her husband and the Papal Nuncio that he would not do so. He suggested that she should either return to Rome, the most honourable course, or return to Grenoble.

Deeply dejected by the King's refusal, Marie proudly wrote a note to be delivered immediately by the Duc de Léqui. asking for his permission to enter the Abbey of Lys, a convent near Melun about two hours journey from Fontainebleau. Louis considered it a great favour when he granted his permission, sending at the same time a messenger with two purses each containing five hundred pistoles. When Marie received the money and a further message from the King that he could not see her, she wittily replied with a touch of asperity in her voice "that she had often heard that people gave ladies' money in order to see them, but never in order not to see them."[4]

Marie was her own worst enemy, though there were many people at Court prepared to do her harm. Colbert, the friend of Madame de Montespan, wrote Madame Colonna that she would be expected to pay the cost of the maintenance of herself and her attendants at the convent out of the money given by the King at Fontainebleau. As Louis had entrusted the Princess Colonna's affairs to his chief minister without her knowledge, she was unwise enough to write him a very querulous letter complaining of the King's lack of consideration. Colbert lost no time in showing Marie's letter to the King. She wrote that "since His Majesty was unwilling to give her liberty to go to Paris he should at least grant her liberty to go anywhere else she might wish."[5] Deeply incensed, 'the Sun King' told Colbert that she must leave the Abbé de Lys and retire to a convent at least sixty leagues from Paris. In despair the wretched Marie implored Colbert for the last time to get Louis to grant her an interview, but she never saw him again. For a few months Marie moved from the Abbey of Avenay near Rheims (a concession granted by Louis since it was only thirty leagues from Paris) to other convents. It was made abundantly clear to her that her continued presence in her beloved France was undesirable. She now decided to ask Charles-Emmanuel of Savoy to give her asylum in his kingdom as her sister had earlier done. Meanwhile Prince Colonna was doing his utmost by fair means or foul to get his wife to return to Italy.

CHAPTER V

Hortense in Chambéry

In many ways the three years Hortense lived in Chambéry were the most agreeable of her life. Her main worry was her pension, because she rarely received it. Possessing a less complicated character than Marie, she was very fortunate, living rent-free in the luxurious Château thanks to the generosity of Charles-Emmanuel and frequently his guest at hunting-parties and balls at Turin.[1] That Hortense and the Duke of Savoy were temporarily lovers, both being essentially sensual, is almost certain, and his wife's dislike of the lovely lady would suggest that she was aware of their liaison. There is no doubt that Hortense enjoyed herself enormously in Chambéry, indulging in her unique way in every gaiety. Her elderly admirer St. Evrémond's subsequent impression of her spending all her time in study and philosophical reflection is completely ludicrous and false.

She was now twenty-six, witty and extremely lively company, not particularly intellectual and a born hostess. At Chambéry she developed her deeper nature and a love of literature and art, marked features of her character later in London. She possessed country tastes; not only did she enjoy hunting, shooting and boating, but she delighted in the entertainments provided by the players and musicians who passed through Chambéry.

When Marie arrived in Piedmont at the end of January 1673, the Duke of Savoy received her most warmly, arranging that she should be allotted the best apartments at the Convent of the Visitation in Turin. Knowing that the Princess Colonna had little money, he delicately hinted that he would like to be her Treasurer if she lacked money. "That is all I possess" said Marie, impulsively showing him the pearls she constantly wore round her neck. "It is the necklace, a present from the King when I parted from him to go to Brouage."

Even in winter it was very gay in Turin, especially when the surrounding country was deep in snow and Charles-Emmanuel and his duchess took part in the sleigh-races. Since poor Marie living in her convent was unable to participate in this diversion, he arranged that one of these sleigh-races should take place under the walls of the convent. It was largely owing to him that the Princess Colonna was granted various amenities. Though much intrigued by Marie's enigmatic character, and fascinated by her charm and wilfulness, there is no real indication they ever became lovers. That probably explains why the Duchess of Savoy Marie-Jeanne always treated Marie in a most friendly way, whereas she resented Charles-Emmanuel's relations with Hortense.

It was natural for Marie to want to visit Hortense in Chambéry, to confide in her and discuss her problems. However, the Duchesse Mazarin behaved in a callous, selfish manner, in contrast to the kindess Marie had shown Hortense on her first arrival in Italy, when fleeing from her husband. This behaviour shows her in a most unfavourable light. Fearing lest any invitation extended to Marie might compromise her own interests with King Louis, she conveniently remembered that she had once made a vow to make a pilgrimage to St. Francis de Sales. Marie felt naturally very aggrieved and upset that Hortense had already departed. What her sister really wanted was to procure the resumption of her pension, and for Louis to regard her part in Marie's flight as favourably as possible.

She therefore wrote to the King from Chambéry (September 12th 1672):

"I do not know, Sire, why my pension is no longer paid to me, and why Your Majesty leaves it to Monsieur Mazarin to give it to me if he chooses. I should never forgive myself if I had brought this on myself, but I did nothing save accompany my sister. She informed you of this, Sire, before we left Rome. If you thought this wrong of me you could have let me know, and I should not have done it. I beseech you, Sire, not to reduce me to the extremity of not knowing where to lay my head. It must be a matter of indifference to you whether Monsieur Mazarin has an extra 24,000 livres on his income or not, and by your intervention you will prevent me from being the unhappiest woman in the world. Be gracious enough to give an answer to him who will present this to you and tell him if you continue it to me."[2]

It is almost incredible that Hortense could hypocritically write to Louis "not to reduce me to the extremity of not knowing where to lay my head" when she knew perfectly well that she was being looked after most generously by Charles-Emmanuel, who to please her constantly showered her with presents. Whether Louis really believed Hortense's cock and bull story is very doubtful, for his own agents in Savoy gave him a different account. Hortense waited for one week before returning to Chambéry, making sure that Marie had departed. She had returned to Turin where she was deeply mortified to hear that the King had given strict orders to the officials of the frontier fortresses to prevent her returning to France. She now turned to the Duke of Savoy, who treated Marie as generously as Hortense, inviting her to hunting-parties and other entertainments at his country house, La Vénerie, when she was able to get permission to leave her convent. Meanwhile her husband continued to send envoys to Savoy to spy on Marie and to report to him her various activities. One envoy made himself such a nuisance that the Prime Minister of Savoy, the Marchese di San Tommasso, declared that no affair of state had given him such annoyance. Eventually it was agreed that the Princess Colonna should be allowed to remain at large for four months provided she did not leave Charles-Emmanuel's dominions. If after four months Marie still refused to return to her husband, she would have to retire to some convent and remain there during the Constable Colonna's good pleasure.

Much of Chambéry, a very ancient town, would be familiar to Hortense Duchesse Mazarin today, the fifteenth century Sainte-Chapel (Holy Chapel), the Porte de la Herse (Portcullis gateway) and the Tour Trésorerie (Treasury Tower) of an even earlier period in the Château. Hortense excelled in horsemanship and she would often go on riding expeditions in the vicinity of Chambéry. As we gaze at the elegant Fountain des Deux Bourneaux today, now over three hundred years old, we remember that it would be new during Hortense's residence in Chambéry. Beautifully situated as the town undoubtedly is, surrounded by mountains and near the exquisite Lac d'Annecy, she honours her most famous citizen, Jean-Jacques Rousseau, rather than the seductive lady, who made such a sensation there in 1672.

Whether or not Charles-Emmanuel remained her lover for more than a few months, he was always fascinated by Hortense's originality, her childishness, her Mancini charm and, above all, by her beauty. Curious as to how she passed the time in Chambéry, the Duke of Savoy sent orders to the Governor d'Orlier to describe to him her manner of life.[3] Hortense was the most amusing company in the world. Life for her was always fun, an everlasting adventure. D'Orlier wrote:

> "She made up a party with Madame Dunoyer (a great friend) and the advocate general, to visit Madame de Leschercine at La Serraz, where the Marquis de la Serraz had a chamois killed in the wood below his house in honour of Madame Mazarin."

> "On Sunday she dressed herself to go to the ball given by the Chevalier de Saint Maurice to Mademoiselle Favier - the dark one (la brune) - in the mall of the château. Nothing more beautiful than Madame could have been seen."

It is curious that his account should depict Hortense as having periodical excesses of religious zeal, for her uncle Cardinal Mazarin, in his lifetime used to reproach her for her irreligion and for not attending mass. "On Sunday," she made her devotion to St. Francis, d'Orlier wrote, and it happens that every time she makes her devotions she does it with so much zeal and fervour that she is ill and remains indisposed for forty-eight hours." "On Monday, she is going to Madame Dunoyer's at Saint Pierre where she will stay for several days to hunt and enjoy herself."

> "When the Duchesse came back from Saint Pierre I gave her Your Royal Highness's letter; she at once told me that she was very sorry she had not answered two letters Your Royal

Highness had written her and thanked you for the wine you sent her. I gave her complimentary messages Your Royal Highness commanded me, and she was very pleased, but when I said that Your Highness would like to be with her, she started to laugh and said that the Constabless (Marie Colonna) had the advantage over her in being in the company of so great a prince."

"Last Saturday Madame Mazarin went with Madame Dunoyer and her groom to the Bois de Candie (a public park in Chambéry). On the return as she was galloping she came off and for two days she has been a little queer (etonée) from her fall."

"On Thursday she confessed to Monsieur Lambert and remained for two hours with him in the Chapel of St. Joseph. Well, if she continues, they will soon have to canonise her. On Monday she spent the whole afternoon with Monsieur d'Arvey and Madame Delarue discussing men's infidelity to women."

"Madame Mazarin has had a rocking-bed (un lit branlant) made in the room next to the Salon; Madame Dunoyer and Monsieur de Villaroses, the advocate-general, rocked themselves with her all day on Sunday. She has learnt with much grief of the death of the Comte de Soissons (her brother-in-law, Olympe's husband). She bathes in her room every morning and three of her favourite nightingales have been eaten by rats."

Here are two interesting aspects of her tastes. Her passion for cleanliness, unusual in the late seventeenth century, and her love of birds.

He refers to her prowess when shooting ducks and geese:

"With a single shot from a pistol-ball she carried off a duck's head. In the afternoon we went to the cornfields at Saint Pierre to look for quails. Madame Mazarin shot one on the wing besides several ortolans and other small birds."

56

"On Tuesday it did nothing but rain; we spent the morning pistol-shooting in a room; a prize of a Crown for the best shot. In the afternoon the weather had improved and we returned to the quail-shooting (à la chasse aux Cailles). Quails well grilled with cheese (fromage pecan[4]) was one of Hortense's favourite dishes. On her return the dogs put up a leveret between Madame Mazarin and Monsieur Delescheraine; they both fired at the same time, and they do not know which of the two killed it." Hortense with her fondness of country life had learnt much country lore. She told her companion that there was nothing more cleansing than leveret's blood, and she at once cut it open, bathing her hands and face with it, and she persuaded Madame Delescheraine to do the same."

The children thought them most odd as they passed through St. Pierre, "all red" and ran after them.

"On Monday we started at dawn to go to the Carthusian Monastery of Alluin with the idea of getting something to eat there. But when the good fathers saw Madame Mazarin, Madame Delescheraine and their maids in the Courtyard they were so terrified that they uttered cries and exclamations which alarmed Madame Mazarin and made her decide not to stop there. The Carthusians recovered from the shock and sent after us a very fine and good collation, which arrived just when it was wanted."

Hortense often attended mass to hear the Bishop of Grenoble preaching, but he made open attacks on comedians and people who attend comedies. After a long talk with her, lasting four hours, she decided to cancel her visit to one of them. This resolution was only temporary because the Duchesse was too fond of the theatre to stay away from them. D'Orlier relates that she attended a performance of Racine's *Bajalet*. Charles-Emmanuel, humouring her every whim, gave her several dogs as presents and she was very attached to them. We hear of her travelling to Aix to get treatment for one of them.

57

"What gave her most pleasure was a present of the Duke of Savoy's, a set of magnificent light firearms exquisitely made. She was like a child, unable to conceal her joy on receiving such a gift."

"She could not weary of looking at them," wrote d'Orlier. Her roguish nature was part of her enchantment, but Charles-Emmanuel found it difficult to take her seriously. During the night she made her maid rise more than six times to bring her arms to her in bed and to observe whether there was something to fire upon in the moonlight."

Hearing that the Duchesse Mazarin was not partial to the local wines, Charles-Emmanuel took the trouble to send her a case of Asti Spumante, the Piedmontese wine, which she much appreciated. She would amuse herself with Madame Delescheraine playing blindman's buff, her favourite game, and roasting chestnuts. These they would drop in the glasses of Asti Spumante they later drank. When Hortense interviewed the cook of one of her friends, the Marquis de Saint-Maurice, she would discuss expertly with her ragouts and entremets. At Hoka, a card game, she usually masked herself, declaring that she did not want anybody to see the faces she made when she lost or won.

When Charles-Emmanuel presented her with a little Moorish boy whose name was Mustapha, Hortense could not conceal her pleasure. According to St. Evrémond he accompanied his mistress later to England. In Chambéry, Mustapha would attend her at fêtes, an imposing little figure walking before her. She was proud of Mustapha and liked to adorn him with caps of Venice point and to teach him French. She would laugh at the silver collar the Moorish boy wore, writing Charles-Emmanuel that the verses he inscribed there were excellent. Like her sister Marie, Hortense was fond of bathing. She often went to Aix to bathe in the lake. The Comte de Cagnol wrote from there:

"Amongst other things she had herself dragged about in the water by her Moor, sometimes on her back, sometimes on her front. This Moor swims like a fish."

He had been captured on a corsair-ship and would remain her faithful servant throughout her life.

D'Orlier's entertaining revelations eventually came to an end because the Duke of Savoy liked to share the more amusing passages with his courtiers. When she heard of this Hortense was so offended that she snubbed d'Orlier on one occasion when he visited her, refusing to see him. D'Orlier was so upset that he wrote to the Duke imploring him to relieve him of this duty.

It was while Hortense was living in Chambéry that her celebrated Mémoires owed their origin. Who was the real author? It is certain that the Duchesse Mazarin provided the material, but the book was almost certainly written by one of her numerous lovers, a rascally adventurer named César Vicard, a native of Chambéry, who called himself the Abbé de St. Réal, though he had no right to this appellation. Hortense collaborated closely with the author, but the work is full of exaggerations, half truths and embellishments.

All her adult life Hortense gloried in publicity, ostentation, and being in the limelight, so that it is hardly convincing when she writes knowingly that "the chief glory of a woman ought to consist of not making herself to be publicly talked of".

Since her adolescence people had done nothing but discuss the lady's eccentric conduct, her fondness for wearing male attire and her love life. To pretend that fate was solely responsible for what happened to her in life and not her highly controversial actions was neither honest nor sincere. If Hortense and Marie were alive today, they would be made much of on television with its penchant for fantasy rather than the truth.

Aged twenty-eight, Hortense was highly experienced in sex, but she had never really lost her heart to any of her lovers. Only in England about seven years later did she fall deeply in love with a Swedish diplomat and his death in extremely tragic circumstances was to cause her intense grief.

After leaving her convent Marie was the guest of the Prince de Carignan, the Comte de Soisson's brother, at his palace. However, on discovering this, the Prince Colonna wrote Marie's host a very indignant letter. When he complained to King Louis, he thought it advisable to write to the Prince de Carignan, a French subject, ordering him to send her away. Marie, now took advantage of the Duke of Savoy's generous invitation to be his guest and that of his wife at La Vénerie, a country house of great beauty surrounded by woodlands and hills. Marie owing to her interest in politics, was able by her charm, intelligence and vivacity to acquire considerable influence over the impressionable Charles-Emmanuel. Every day she received in her apartments the Foreign Ministers and other luminaries. It was almost as if she was back at Fontainebleau, fêted by all the Court.

Unfortunately the dormant demon in this "best and the wildest of the Mazarinettes" (as Saint-Simon called her) soon asserted itself. She was always a slave to her violent passions. Though the Duchess of Savoy never disliked Marie as she did Hortense, she became increasingly aware that the Princess Colonna was acquiring too much influence over Charles-Emmanuel. Knowing his wife's sentiments, the Duke of Savoy suggested to his guest that in order to diminish any suspicions his wife might have formed in her mind, he would recommend occasionally in her presence the advisability of Marie seeking reconciliation with her husband. Apparently Marie misunderstood her host's intentions. When he raised the matter in a casual way one day, she flew into a passion and left the room. Nothing would pacify her, but she eventually on the Duchess's entreaties consented to remain another week. It is charitable to think that Marie had never really recovered from the brain fever that seized her after her forced rejection by King Louis. Her eternal restlessness indicates some mental illness within herself. She should, however, have shown more gratitude to the Duke of Savoy.

Marie gives her own version of this episode in her Mémoires:

"My happiness was too great. Fortune, which delighted in tormenting me, took care not to permit it to last. To interrupt accordingly its course, she inspired His Royal Highness with political sentiments and impelled him one day to propose to me to return to Rome, pointing out that I should be much happier there than in a cloister, and that, if there were any obstacle to my return, besides the ill-feeling between the Constable and myself, he would be the guarantor of our reunion."

60

What a fatal decision to reject the kindly overtures of the Duke and to insist on leaving his dominions.

So, during the autumn (1673), Marie started again on her strange travels, always bringing suffering on herself by her wilfulness and pride. Pursued by the menace of a resentful husband, she was imprisoned for a time in a fortress in Antwerp and treated like a state criminal. Then, accompanied by her faithful Moréna, willing to share all her sufferings because of her devotion to her mistress, she eventually arrived in Spain.

While she remained in Turin, Charles II of England remembering Marie Mancini during his exile in France, had written to her inviting her to England, but Marie did not accept the invitation. She wrote to him from Madrid:[5]

> "I should have given myself the honour of writing to Your Majesty, if I had been able to hope that my letters would have been conveyed to him with all the secrecy that I wished. My desire to retain the kindly sentiments which Your Majesty expressed to me, while I was at Turin and my fear that you have been prejudiced against me, impels me to ask you for their confirmation. Send it to me, I entreat you, since I could receive nothing more opportune or more agreeable in the state in which I find myself. But let Your Majesty accompany it with secrecy, since there is nothing of more importance and since the good or ill success of my affairs depends upon it absolutely as I depend upon Your Majesty, being all my life his most humble and very obedient servant."

She was anxious for his friendship and hoped that he would help her.

Olympe, Comtesse de Soissons, Superintendent of Louis's Spanish Queen's household after her marriage, made use of her influential position by relentless intrigues. She was not particularly clever, being called "The Soissons goose" at the French Court and more often "Madame La Comtesse". Renowned for her love affairs like all the Mancini sisters, though none of her paramours seemed permanently attached to her. Eugène Maurice Prince of Savoy-Carignan Comte de Soissons seemed devoted to her, though conveniently enough for her a complacent husband. Jealous of Henriette Duchesse d'Orleans's (Charles II of England's youngest sister) political influence with King Louis, she malevolently tried her utmost to harm both Henriette - known as Madame - and Louise de la Vallière, the King's early mistress. Olympe was mistress for a while of the Marquis de Vardes, a handsome scoundrel with a magnificent head, leonine in its great wig.[6] When de Vardes, prompted by vanity, attempted to make love to Madame (the Duchesse d'Orléans), Olympe became very jealous and by way of retaliation accused Madame's devoted admirer the Comte de Guiche fighting valiantly in Poland of the grossest treachery. Meanwhile de Vardes, despicably betrayed to King Louis the contents of a confidential letter Madame had unwisely entrusted to him for transmission to her brother Charles in England.

Piqued because Madame Henriette had rejected his advances, he next proceeded to make disparaging remarks about her in the presence of the Chevalier de Lorraine, her husband's favourite. For her part in these odious intrigues, the Comtesse de Soissons was banished to Champagne together with her husband, who was the Governor of the province of Champagne. He at least was innocent of any participation in this affair. On being allowed to return to Paris, Olympe resumed her office as Superintendent of the Queen's household, but never regained her former influence. To console herself for the loss of de Vardes, who after being consigned to the Bastille and the citadel of Montpellier, was banished to Aigues-Mortes in Provence, Olympe took as her lover the Marquis de Villeroi, nicknamed by the ladies "le Charmant".

There in the Hôtel de Soissons she indulged in her pleasures and intrigues. When Olympe's husband died mysteriously in Champagne (May 1673) many people said that the Comte de Soissons had died of poison handed to him by an agent of his wife. Others, knowing she dabbled in sorcery, witchcraft and astrology, ascribed his death to the occult. Her younger son, Prince Eugène of Savoy, born in Paris on October 18th 1663 and rather neglected by his mother in his boyhood, was to become a soldier of genius.

Hortense's youngest sister Marianne, who so delighted her uncle and Queen Anne of Austria with her childish verses, maintained her interest in literature all her life. She was known as an

62

important patroness of poets, particularly as the inspiration for La Fontaine's *Fables*. She and her husband the Duc de Bouillon were poles apart and he was often absent engrossed in his military career. On one occasion before setting out for the wars in Hungary, the Duc de Bouillon extremely reluctant to leave Marianne alone in Paris, implored her to stay during his absence in their own Duchy of Château-Thierry in Champagne on the Marne. There she met the ranger of the neighbouring forests, Jean de la Fontaine, who finding her personality pleasing and attractive and no doubt thinking she could assist his literary career, paid assiduous court to her.[7] The Duchesse de Bouillon's delicate mind and playful spirit were very congenial to the poet, and it was under her supervision that the first six books of his *Fables* were published. Marianne surnamed La Fontaine "le Fablier" and felt instinctively where his true genius lay. He took pleasure in her witty, animated conversation and eulogized her in his poetry.

Like all the Mancini sisters except Laure, the Duchesse de Bouillon was notorious for her love affairs. When her husband discovered that she had been responding too ardently to the advances of the Comte de Louvigay, younger son of the Maréchal de Grammont, he decided during 1675 after many entreaties from his family, to send Marianne to the Convent de Montreuil "to give her an opportunity for salutary reflections". After a few months she returned to Paris, more light-hearted than ever in her accounts of her adventures in the Convent.

Marianne was almost as interested in necromancy, astrology and the occult as Olympe and they were both later implicated during 1679 in a fearful scandal, the notorious L'Affaire des Poisons.

CHAPTER VI

An Excess of Folly

Hortense was never in the least politically minded, happy enough in Savoy during the summer (1675), indulging in her pleasures, taking advantage of Charles-Emmanuel's generosity and good nature and taking no thought for the morrow. If she occasionally remembered her former suitor Charles II, she had little knowledge of what was transpiring in England, nor did she much care. She would have known that France and the United Provinces were at war, and that England was also involved. She would have heard that the Bretonne Louise de Keroualle Duchess of Portsmouth was Charles's reigning mistress, but she would not have troubled her head whether the French lady had acquired much influence or not. She was, of course, absolutely unaware that Louise's enemies in London were seeking opportunities to supplant her by another woman, hoping that French influence would be diminished.

It was far from easy to find a woman dazzling enough to achieve their purpose. Halifax (George Savile first Marquis of), who knew Charles II intimately, wrote that it was decided by others whom he should have in his arms, but he sometimes chose for himself.[1] Some time during the summer of 1675 the Duchess of Portsmouth's bitter enemy Ralph Montagu, a former ambassador in France, and his sister Lady Harvey, were considering Hortense Mazarin as a candidate, whom they thought possessed the ripe beauty and intelligence to excite the senses of the sated monarch.

Then Charles-Emmanuel died suddenly during June 1675, and his son being a minor, his widow Marie-Jeanne became regent. Hortense might have stayed indefinitely in Chambéry, but Marie-Jeanne - Madame de Savoie as she was called - had old scores to pay and soon showed the Duchesse Mazarin that she was no longer welcome in Savoy. She ordered Hortense to leave the country and even informed the Duc Mazarin that he could have his wife arrested within the territory of Savoy if he so desired. Women are sometimes more revengeful than men and have longer memories.

It would seem that something providential constantly turned up in Hortense's life in her dire extremity. Ralph Montagu, an able diplomat, but unscrupulous intriguer, who had been present as a young ambassador to France at the death-bed of the Duchess of Orléans (Charles II's Minette), arrived in Savoy with an invitation for Hortense. She would be a very welcome guest at the Court of St. James's. Montagu calculated that Louise Duchess of Portsmouth's influence with Charles was waning, and considered that she would be no match for the lovely Duchesse Mazarin. He advised Hortense to make her own arrangements for travel as if she had determined to settle in England of her own accord. It is very likely that Hortense rather than luring Charles II into her toils favoured England for personal reasons. Her Italian-born cousin Maria Beatrice d'Este, daughter of the Duke of Modena and Laure Martinozzi, was now the second wife of James Duke of York, heir presumptive to the throne. Surely she would be given a warm welcome in London.

With her characteristic love of adventure, Hortense leapt at Ralph Montagu's suggestion. Dressed as a cavalier, "on horseback and wearing a plumed hat, and a peruke", she left Chambéry accompanied by a groom, four valets, two maids and Mustapha. One of Hortense's greatest qualities was her extraordinary courage. Fearing that she might be arrested on French soil she decided to travel through countries where wars were raging; Switzerland, Alsace and Germany, escorted by twenty horsemen. Exhilarated by the fresh air, the long days in the saddle, Hortense thought nothing of the danger. Expertly and fearlessly, she rode over mountain passes, through sweet-smelling meadows and dense forests, sleeping where she could lay her head, the warm summer air caressing her face. She did not mind at all that in order to reach Amsterdam and Brill to embark on a boat for England, she had to cross the Low Countries ravaged by war.

Sidonia Marquise de Courcelles - that lovely butterfly - mentioned Hortense in one of her letters[2] written November 8th 1675 to her lover du Boulay in Geneva. Her former friendship with Hortense - alas! - no more. "On arriving here," she wrote,

"I learnt that Madame Mazarin had passed several days here before retiring to Germany in a town which is called, I believe, Augsburg . . . This was because Madame de Savoie immediately after her husband's death commanded her to leave her territories. Some say that it was a scruple on the part of Madame de Savoie who does not wish to give her protection to one who has quarrelled with her husband and is suspected of bad conduct, others that it was during the life of the Duke, she felt jealousy towards the Mazarin who when she was in favour had often behaved insolently to her. This seems the most credible reason, however, it is most unfortunate to find oneself driven away from every place. But what is most strange is that this woman triumphs over all her misfortunes by an excess of folly which has no parallel and that after receiving this setback she thinks only of enjoying herself. When passing through here she was on horseback, befeathered and bewigged, escorted by twenty men. She talked of nothing but violins and of hunting-parties and everything else that gives pleasure."

The venom in her words "this woman triumphs over all her misfortunes", reveals that Sidonia now disliked Hortense. Running away with her latest lover, Sidonia can neither conceal her envy or her malice, for Hortense had already achieved considerable fame and notoriety whereas her own Mémoires had received comparatively little notice. She mentions her again on November 22nd. "The Mazarin has left Augsburg on the way to Munich in Bavaria."

When she encountered difficulties at the various frontiers, the Duchesse Mazarin used her beautiful eyes to such effect on the Customs Officers that they let her pass. Taking a wild joy in all her adventures, Hortense with her entourage moved on to Amsterdam where Polastron sent by her husband awaited her with orders to arrest her, but she managed to elude him. It was already December 1675 when the Duchesse Mazarin accompanied by Saint-Réal, her current lover, by Mustapha her little Moor, possibly by Nanon and other servants, embarked at Brill for England. It was a very rough passage. The boat in which she was travelling was driven out of her course, and Hortense was forced to land at Sole Bay. In many ways the Italianate lady was born before her time, particularly in her taste for male costume. In this guise she rode on horseback to London accompanied by her seven servants. When she was within easy access of that City having been met by Ralph Montagu, he accompanied her up Bedford Street as far as Covent Garden where his sister Lady Elizabeth Harvey's house had been temporarily taken for her.

One wonders whether she was sincere, though even the usually indefatigable Hortense must have been exhausted after her travel, when she told Montagu that she wanted to remain incognito. Hardly unexpected considering the Duchesse's fame and notoriety, the piazza was soon crowded with people avid to catch a glimpse of her. Her arrival caused a great sensation, for rumours spread that political intrigues were responsible for it. The Marquis de Ruvigni, an elderly aristocrat and leader of the French Protestants, was serving then as ambassador in London. He soon paid Hortense a visit, but departed to pay his respects to the politically minded Duchess of Portsmouth in Whitehall. Louise de Keroualle already felt distinct qualms as to Hortense's intention, fearing that her established position as *maîtresse en titre* might be in jeopardy. Mary Beatrice, the young Duchess of York, now aged eighteen, hastened to invite her cousin Hortense to one of her receptions, for she strongly disliked the French favourite.

In France and other parts of Europe speculation abounded as to the reasons for the Duchesse's arrival in London. Writing to her daughter on Christmas Day 1675 the Marquise de Sévigné is full of gossip. She wrote:

"Madam de Mazarin for her part is rambling about the wide world. It is thought she is in England, where you know there is neither faith nor law, nor priest, but I believe it is not true as it is said in the song, that she is for driving out the King from thence."[3]

If Ralph Montagu was primarily responsible for Hortense's coming to London, Charles Marguetel de St. Denis, Seigneur de St. Evrémond, an exile in England for many years, had also been instrumental in persuading her to accept Montagu's invitation. He had known Hortense as a child in France and now welcomed her eagerly to London. For about fourteen years this elderly philosopher and man of letters had been living there in exile, having made injudicious criticism of Cardinal Mazarin at the time of the Treaty of the Pyrenees. In his portrait in the National Portrait Gallery by J. Parmentier St. Evrémond appears rather ugly, an enormous wen covering his face between his two eyes. Very tall, he wore a cap over his white hair, preferring it to the then fashionable periwig. His friends delighted in his wit, culture and brilliant conversation. Charles II liked him, creating him Keeper of the King's ducks in St. James's Park and giving him a small salary. St. Evrémond became deeply devoted to Hortense, an elderly man realistic enough to know that partly because of his age - he had been born in 1613 - he stood no chance with her as a lover. Yet in his correspondence we become aware how much he loved Hortense. Henceforward this was the most important friendship in her life.

She was now aged twenty-nine. Southern women age quickly, but Hortense retained her pagan beauty. She was writes one of her lovers, probably Saint-Réal[4] "one of those lofty Roman beauties, no way like our baby-visaged and puppet-like faces of France" (a sly reference to the Duchess of Portsmouth). People were intrigued by the colour of her eyes:

> "It is neither blue, nor gray, nor altogether black, but a mixture of all three, which participates of all the excellence that is found in them. They have the sweetness of the blue, the briskness of the gray and above all, the fire of the black."

Hortense had first met her Martinozzi cousin, the young graceful Duchess of York, James's second wife[5] then only fifteen, when she visited her in Chambéry. Maria d'Este was on her way from Modena to marry James. A reluctant bride in 1673, she found consolation in a visit to the Sisters of the Visitation Convent, although later she grew to love him. Now Hortense was given a lodging by the Duke and Duchess of York in St. James's Palace. Mary of Modena was *enceinte*, and her brother-in-law, who was fond of her, was in the habit of visiting her where there were plenty of opportunities to talk to the Duchesse Mazarin in the Duchess of York's bedchamber. At first Hortense's conduct seems to have been exemplary, but she soon discussed with the King her marriage difficulties and her pension, so persuasively indeed that both Charles and James wrote to King Louis requesting him to increase it.

Although Charles was not at first particularly attracted to Hortense, it was not long before the Marquis de Ruvigny was writing to Louis:

> "I have just learnt that there is a certain and very secret intelligence (understanding) between the King of England and Madam Mazarin. She carries on her intrigue very quietly."[6]

The ambassador was increasingly uneasy that Louise de Keroualle Duchess of Portsmouth might be eclipsed by the Duchesse Mazarin, for Louise was a vital link between the two kings. She was the most hated of his mistresses, partly because people in England realized she was working in the French interest and many suspected that she was a French spy. Her innate strength lay in her subtle understanding of Charles's character and peculiar needs. Avaricious by nature and dominated by motives of self-interest, self-preservation and self-aggrandisement, her unpopularity was also owing to the Francophobia prevalent in Stuart England, though many at Court favoured France and aped French ways. Louise was a woman of taste and refinement, a complete contrast to Nell Gwyn, who took every opportunity to deride the French favourite.

This great comic actress's most lovable qualities such as her warm-heartedness and essential kindness appeal to us today even more than they did to her friends in her lifetime of thirty-seven years. Possibly we have too sentimental a view of this enchanting creature. She was extremely witty and humorous, capable of malice, giddy, coarse, and ambitious, and possessed a frankness that was wholly admirable. She often scored off the Duchess of Portsmouth.

When Nell one day appeared in a rich dress, Louise said slightly contemptuously, "Nelly, you are grown rich, I believe by

your dress. Why, woman you are fine enough to be a Queen."
"You are entirely right, Madam" retorted Nell, "and I am whore
enough to be a Duchess."[7] She called the King her 'Charles the
third', because two previous lovers, Charles Hart the actor and
Lord Buckhurst a nobleman poet, had both borne the same name.
Let the King have an affair with the Roman lady, she thought,
sure that her Charles would always return to her for fun and fro-
lics. She was intelligent enough to know that Portsmouth was her
real rival.

When Charles did not offer Louise any lodging during a visit
to Newmarket, she was extremely dejected and because she felt ill
and jaded, left the Court to retire to Bath, then becoming fashionable, to take the waters, where she remained from May 25th till
July 4th. In London she was often in tears, complaining bitterly to
Ruvigny how badly the King treated her, but Nell merely jibed at
her, calling her 'the Weeping Willow' or 'Squintabella', because of
a cast in her eye. Her enemies exulted too soon at Louise's supposed downfall and Nell went into mock mourning.

During the Spring (1676) King Louis decided that another
diplomat, a little dapper elderly Norman named Honoré de Courtin, with a real talent for petticoat diplomacy, should be sent to
London, firstly for the purpose of cooperating with Ruvigny and
then to succeed him as Ambassador. The appointment was an ideal
one in the prevailing circumstances in Charles II's Court, for he
was very much a ladies man, an accomplished, hardworking diplomat, courtly with a subtle Gallic wit, who concealed his considerable ability under a veneer of indolence and frivolity. His despatches to his friends Pomponne, the Foreign Minister, and to
Louvois, are delightful in their subtlety and psychological insight.

Louis was aware that the Duchesse Mazarin had created a
great stir in Charles II's Court and that the King had been attracted
by her beauty. So far the affair had been conducted with some
secrecy, but Courtin considered "that it likely that the growing
passion will take the first place in the heart of that prince". What
worried Louis were Hortense's real sentiments towards himself,
since he suspected that she did not bear him sufficient gratitude
for what he had done for her. She had begged him to force the
Duc Mazarin to increase to twenty thousand crowns the pension

of eight thousand crowns which Louis wanted to give her, but the King did not consider that he was justified to act in such a way until such time she was willing to return to her husband. He feared lest his negative attitude towards her might annoy the lady, causing her to use her influence against him with the King of England. Meanwhile Monsieur Courtin was instructed to assure Hortense that King Louis bore her good will, and that later on she might expect to benefit by his protection and kindness.[8] This sort of petticoat diplomacy was very congenial to Courtin.

At the same time he was told to treat the Duchess of Portsmouth with great respect, although reports from London insisted that her influence had declined. After Harry Savile, a bachelor rake and accomplished diplomat, often at Court, reported to his intimate friend the poet-earl of Rochester in the country that Louise was out of favour during April 1676, Rochester wrote magnanimously to Savile, though he disliked her:

> "I am sorry for the declining D. Louise and would have you generous to her at this time for that is True Pride, and I delight in it."[9]

By the summer many people were convinced that Hortense was King Charles's mistress. The shrewd, well-informed Courtin noticed that the King was often absent from his apartments in Whitehall, and thought he was sleeping with the Duchesse Mazarin. There was nothing elevated about the affair. For the time being the King was infatuated with her physical beauty, and her personal fascination, her hazardous adventures and her conversation appealed to him enormously.

Neither Charles nor Hortense, however, were capable of fidelity in their love relationship for long. He gave many entertainments for her both on land and on the Thames, for the weather was warm and caressing, made for dalliance and laughter. When Charles went up the river during the evenings to bathe, Hortense did not accompany him, much as she would have enjoyed mixed bathing, but it was not indulged in at Charles II's Court. Courtin wrote a trifle cynically to King Louis: "It is the only decency which they observe in this country. There is a great deal of laxness in the rest of their conduct."

71

On July 5th, the day after her return from Bath, the Duchess of Portsmouth went by coach to dine with King Charles at Windsor, but she was full of chagrin when not invited to stay the night. Courtin reported to his master that the sojourn in Bath had vastly improved her health. He wrote: "but she is still a little thin. She hopes that by resting to become plump again." Charles's name for her was Fubbs and he called a yacht after her.

According to Courtin, Nell Gwyn indulged in her customary mockery of her rival. He would refer to her as "Mistris Nesle" when writing to his Foreign Minister. The actress affected to be greatly alarmed at the Duchess of Portsmouth's return, declaring that she would arm herself to the teeth to protect herself against the resentment which would be bound to fall on her owing to the frequent visits Charles had paid her during the absence of the official mistress.[10]

Louise's jealousy was fully aroused when shortly after her return to London she gave a sumptuous farewell banquet for Ruvigny, who was returning to France. After dinner three of King Louis's musicians La Forest, Gandomeche and Gilet, gave a concert. What amused the courtiers most was Louise calling for a Spanish song as Charles entered her magnificent apartments in Whitehall: "Mat ne con non mirar mas mo mate me con celos".[11]

So, the Court watched intrigued, diverted by the contrast between the two rival Duchesses, and the Comedian Nell Gwyn. Edmund Waller, who knew Hortense well, and famous for his lovely song "Go, lovely Rose", wrote his rhymed couplets relating the rivalry of the three Sultanas. It is called *The Triple Combat*:

> "When thro' the world fair Mazarine had run,
> Bright as her fellow-traveller the sun,
> Hither at length the Roman eagle flies,
> As the last triumph of her conqu'ring eyes . . .
> But Portsmouth, springing from the antient race
> of Britons, which the Saxon here did chase,
> As they great Caesar did oppose, makes head,
> And does against this new invader lead . . .
>
> What may the Fates design! For never yet
> From distant regions two such beauties met.

Venus had been an equal friend to both,
And Vict'ry to declare herself seems loath;
Over the camp with doubtful wings she flies;
Till Chloris shining in the field she spies.
The lovely Chloris well attended came,
A thousand Graces waited on the dame;
Her matchless form made all the English glad,
And foreign Beauties less assurance had."

'The lovely Chloris' is probably Nell Gwyn, possibly Jane Middleton, considered by Honoré de Courtin, no mean judge, the greatest beauty at Charles II's Court. Edmund Waller lived near the Duchesse Mazarin for some years in St. James's.

CHAPTER VII

The Rival Sultanas

Hortense enjoyed herself enormously in London during the summer and autumn (1676), sometimes accompanying the Duke of Buckingham (George Villiers second Duke) to Bartholomew Fair, much frequented by fashionable courtiers. This gifted unstable nobleman, "everything by fits and nothing long", was no friend of Louise's. She never forgave him for keeping her waiting as a young girl at Dieppe, seemingly having forgotten her very existence, before coming to London and eventually becoming King Charles's mistress.

Hortense was as attractive to members of her own sex as to the many males enamoured of her. She formed a great friendship with the young Countess of Sussex, Charles's illegitimate daughter by Barbara Duchess of Cleveland, now in France. Anne Fitzroy scarcely more than a child was infatuated with the lovely Hortense, and her passionate sentiments certainly had a lesbian quality. She now occupied apartments formerly used by her mother immediately above King Charles's apartments. Married when very young to the stupid but upright Earl of Sussex, she preferred Court life to life in the country. It was very convenient for Charles to make assignations with the Duchesse Mazarin in his daughter's apartments. When this came to the ears of the Duchess of Portsmouth she was absolutely desolate, blaming Lady Sussex for her compliance in the matter. In such a way did she make a powerful enemy. Sometimes Charles saw Hortense in Lady Harvey's house - another of her friends and considered by Courtin "the most intriguing and the cleverest woman in England".

Her brother Ralph Montagu's sole object in encouraging the affair was to destroy the Duchess of Portsmouth's influence. He did not want Hortense to acquire any political ascendancy, nor was there any danger of this, for Charles seldom allowed himself to be ruled by his mistresses. In any case political affairs held no interest for Hortense Mazarin.

Courtin wrote in his entertaining way to his Foreign Minister Pomponne, "As you desire to know how I am in England, I may tell you that up to now the air has not done me any harm." He liked to chaff his friend, for he had known him in boyhood. The only thing he disliked about England was its climate, and he complained about the damp coldness to King Charles, who liking him, advised him to wear a special kind of flannel vest to resist the cold.

Courtin occupied a house, Number 8 York Street off St. James's Square, now becoming fashionable. "Madame Mazarin is coming to dine with me today with the Countess of Sussex" he wrote. Anne Fitzroy born in 1661 was now fifteen. A frequent visitor was Jane Middleton, who had lovely auburn hair, an exquisite figure and a host of admirers, including Ralph Montagu and the poet Edmund Waller. Jane, daughter of Sir Robert Needham, had married Charles Middleton of Ruabon in 1660, but was unfaithful to him. Ralph Montagu was her most ardent lover, but Courtin told his Foreign Minister that "he had fallen into Madame Mazarin's toils". This is most unlikely because Montagu's interest in Hortense was political.

The ambassador liked to ramble in St. James's Park on warm summer nights. There he would meet his colleague Don Luis de Vasconcellos Conde de Castelmethor, "dying for love of Madam Mazarin". Her indifference to him seemed the height of cruelty. Charles II stocked the canal in St. James's Park with water-fowl, and John Evelyn in his Diary (February 9th 1664-1665) mentions "a melancholy water-fowl brought from Astracan by the Russian Ambassador". There were not only birds, but deer, antelopes and sheep. We think of Charles most affable of monarchs sauntering in the park with his spaniels and feeding his ducks. Nobody really knows how Birdcage Walk derived its name. It is thought that the King had the cages of his favourite birds hung from the trees, but there is no proof of this in the prints of the period.[1]

The Duchesse Mazarin was very familiar with St. James's Park, for together with Lady Sussex she would practise fencing there, but Thomas Lennard her husband resented his wife's friendship with the beautiful Hortense.

Though he might feign to be a dilettante, Courtin feared that Hortense, unless King Louis humoured her over her pension, might side with the party most hostile to France. He worked extremely hard to frustrate this: "You know better than I do," he wrote his Foreign Minister,

> "that the whole English nation is filled with animosity against France, that the Lord Treasurer (Danby, a former friend of the Duchess of Portsmouth), the one amongst the Ministers who had most influence over the King, appears at any rate to affect the same sentiments to the point even of not caring to call on me as he should have done. Nothing remains for us but to set against us the person who has most influence over the King's heart."[2]

Meanwhile the dapper little diplomat was careful to remain on excellent terms with both Louise and Hortense. When he visited Louise in Whitehall at the beginning of August, he found her very desolate, fearful that her reign was over as *maîtresse en titre*. "Yesterday evening," he wrote Pomponne,

> "I saw something which aroused all my pity and which would perhaps have touched you, wise and serious as you are . . . Madame de Portsmouth explained to me what grief the frequent visits of the King of England to Madame de Sussex cause her every day . . . I remained with her till midnight and omitted nothing to ease her mind and show her what interest she had in concealing her grief" . . .

Louis was amused by his ambassador's despatches, especially when he referred to Louise as "the Signora Adolorada". All the same what alarmed him most was the possibility of the eclipse of Portsmouth, the chain by which he had bound Charles to him.[3] If this should materialize, a party antagonistic to his interests would emerge in England. As the King of France was anxious for a separate peace with Holland, he gave instructions to his diplomats at the Congress of Nimuegen that there had been no decline in the influence of the Duchess of Portsmouth with King Charles. This was only partly true.

In Courtin's opinion it was necessary to be *un homme de plaisir* to get anywhere in England, and his work was at least made more pleasurable by his zest for the society of the lovely ladies who adorned Charles II's Court. He was richly amused when Nell Gwyn merrily told him that if the King of France felt inclined to continue making valuable presents to the King of England's mistress (Louise) they could be in future made more fitly to her.[4] He certainly did not take her seriously, knowing that "the frisking comedian" had no political influence whatsoever. He was delighted when various ladies present had not the slightest difficulty in persuading Nelly to allow them to inspect her under garments, writing M. Pomponne:

> "Never in my life did I see such cleanliness, neatness and sumptuousness. I should speak of certain other things which were shown to all of us, if M. de Lionne were still Foreign Secretary, but with you Sir, I must be more grave and decorous."

Pomponne, however, was human enough to tell his friend:

> "I am sure you forgot all your troubles when you were making Mistress Nesle raise those neat and magnificent petticoats of hers."

There was a great deal of gambling at Court, particularly the new fashionable card game basset, introduced into England by the croupier Morin. Hortense was sometimes fortunate, for she won 1,400 guineas at basset playing against Nell Gwyn and on another occasion 5,000 pounds.[5] St. Evrémond always declared that the Duchesse Mazarin was capable of cheating in the Italian fashion if she was losing and Hortense would have been candid enough to agree with him. However, Nell's invectives might have caused some raised eyebrows if Madame Mazarin had cheated when playing with her. Courtin does not relate whether he lost at 'l'ombre', another very popular card game, when playing with Hortense. Louvois, by nature licentious, wrote to his friend:

> "I don't know the first card in ombre, so that all I could have done would have been to fasten my eyes on Madame Mazarin."

Charles himself never cared for cards, nor did he possess any real enthusiasm for gambling. During his exile he had occasionally wiled away weary hours playing cards with cronies such as Harry Bennet (later Earl of Arlington) and Henry Wilmot Earl of Rochester, father of the poet-rake. Like many naturally generous men he hated losing, and he often did. He had once written despondently to the Duke of Ormonde: "God sende you better lucke at pickett than I have with Harry Bennet at cribbage."

Charles Cotton in his fascinating book *The Complete Gamester* wrote of gaming in general: "Gaming is an enchanting witchery, gotten betwixt idleness and avarice, an itching disease, that makes some scratch the head whilst others, as if they were bitten by a tarantula are laughing themselves to death"... According to Charles Cotton, Charles II was often taken in by the Duchesse Mazarin when he played with her, though he was by nature so shrewd that one may reasonably doubt it. Though Hortense usually played fairly at cards, she was capable of cheating, "playing altogether upon the sharp" at any game of chance, if she suspected her opponent of sharp play. Since several of his mistresses were neither so clever or fortunate at cards as Hortense, Charles certainly grudged them losing money, well aware as he was that he would have to pay their debts.

During the early days of the Restoration the most popular game of chance was ombre, a game of Spanish origin, thought to have been introduced into England by Catherine of Braganza and much liked by her. By 1677 when Hortense was in London, basset, a French game, had displaced ombre as the most fashionable game of chance, indulged in by the Court where high play was possible and by no means confined to libertines, for noblemen of the highest integrity such as the Duke of Ormonde were great gamblers. During the twenty-three years Hortense spent in London (until her death) the mania for gambling had reached its zenith. The games of chance most favoured by the French were lansquenet, piquet and ombre, and because it was undoubtedly risky and extravagant, basset was eventually forbidden in France except in the houses of foreign ambassadors.

Reports that Hortense was as witty and humorous in her maturity as she was undoubtedly beautiful had now reached

France. Louvois chaffed Courtin that he had fallen for Madame Mazarin, another victim, but the Ambassador hastened to reassure him that it was not true. He was far from insensible to her charms, however, finding her tantalizing enough when he watched her dancing the furlana to the guitar, like a Neapolitan gypsy. In their wildness, their sudden change of mood and spontaneous gaiety Hortense and Marie were unmistakedly of the South.

Like her friend the Duke of Buckingham, Hortense was a brilliant mimic, never failing to amuse Courtin. Once when he happened to be at her lodging, news of the capture of Valenciennes by King Louis's armies was brought to him. "Madame Mazarin is already training to be a news-hawker," he wrote Louvois.

> "She stalked up and down the four rooms that compose her little lodging, passing and repassing me and crying in a news-hawkers voice 'Capture of Valenciennes by the King's army, commanded by His Majesty'. Several times I felt inclined to curse the hawker."

Although Courtin sympathized with the Duchesse rather than with her husband, he constantly advised that she must be induced to return to France.

Courtin had real genius for petticoat diplomacy. He conceived the brilliant idea of asking Hortense and Louise to supper with him with the object of reconciling them, although well aware that both ladies detested one another. It so happened that he met the intriguing Lady Harvey and Jane Middleton at the theatre one day, and took the opportunity to suggest that they should bring Hortense and Louise soon for dinner to the Embassy. His diplomacy achieved its purpose. The food was delicious and the wine excellent. However, his way of trying to effect a reconciliation between the two ladies was very curious, for he locked them both in a closet. To everybody's surprise they eventually emerged laughing and skipping. Such a friendship could hardly be sincere, but Louise and Hortense henceforward occasionally accompanied each other in a coach. Perhaps Louise now realized that her rival, she was volatile and mercurial by nature, would not remain dangerous for long.

Louise continued to nag King Charles, complaining that Lady Sussex was the intermediary in his liaison with Hortense. Meanwhile the former Lady Castlemaine, now Duchess of Cleveland, wrote abusive letters from France both to Charles and her daughter, threatening to come over and remove Anne to Paris unless she returned to her husband in the country and abandoned Hortense. Barbara Cleveland, the most wanton of Charles's ex-mistresses, was hardly in a position to preach morality to her daughter. In their quarrel the King continued to support Anne in defying her mother. Unfortunately the fondness of Hortense and the Countess for fencing in St. James's Park attracted too much publicity and gossip. As Lady Chaworth mentions in a letter to her brother Lord Roos,

> "they went downe into St. James's Park the other day with drawne swords under their night gowns, which they drew out and made successful fine passes with, much to the admiration of severall men that was lookers-on in the Parke."[6]

Even her father was reluctantly forced to take action, insisting largely owing to Barbara's pestering, that Anne must join her husband in his country seat of Hurstmonceux Castle in Sussex. Lord Sussex was threatening a formal separation unless she gave up Madame Mazarin and went to live with him in the country.[7] He considered that the Duchesse Mazarin's influence on Anne had been harmful. During November they attended the Lord Mayor's Show together, and whilst looking on the spectacle from their balcony in Cheapside, some badly disposed persons had hurled a volley of squibs, almost putting out Anne's eye.[8] So the poor girl returned to Hurstmonceux Castle where for a while she desperately pined for the beautiful Hortense. At night she would continually gaze at the portrait of her friend and lavish it with kisses. Even the pleasures of country life, hunting the hare or the fox, though it improved her health could not make her forget Hortense. It is unlikely, however, that Hortense, basking in Charles's favour and surrounded by lovers, real and potential, missed the Countess of Sussex very much. The Earl might make his young wife pregnant

80

again - she had already lost one infant, but she had little in common with her unimaginative, but well-meaning husband. Later we find her in France, succeeding her mother as Ralph Montagu's mistress, perhaps a kind of revenge for Barbara's earlier interference in her marital affairs.

Two men were mainly responsible for encouraging Hortense to take an eager interest in literature, art and philosophy, interests first acquired in Chambéry. St. Réal, who had collaborated with her when writing her Mémoires, was a rascal, but a very cultured man. He had collected for her an excellent library, but he was jealous of her friendships with other men, sometimes sitting sullen and brooding in front of a fire in her apartments without saying a word. When the handsome Prince of Monaco, a friend of Hortense's in Chambéry, visited London during October 1676, she gave him a cordial welcome. It was now that St. Réal made up his mind to leave England. Courtin told Pomponne that

> "Madame Mazarin sustained his departure with the fortitude of a Roman matron, and to tell you the truth I am greatly deceived if she is not very pleased at being delivered from him."

St. Evrémond, who knew everybody worth knowing in London society, introduced her to philosophers, literary personalities and even learned canons. Hortense's apartments in St. James became the centre for distinguished foreigners visiting England, and all sorts of serious discussions on literature and art took place there.

During July Hortense's former friend Sidonia de Courcelles arrived in England, probably with the object of attracting the attention of the King. England was then a haven for all the women who had quarrelled with their husbands. Sidonia certainly had no false modesty about her charms. She relates in her Mémoires:

> "I am tall. I have an admirable figure. My eyes are rather large and I never open them fully, which is a charm that gives me the sweetest and tenderest look imaginable. My throat is well modelled, my hands divine, my arms passable, that is to say a little thin, but I am consoled for this misfor-

tune by the pleasure of having the most beautiful legs in the world."

Perhaps Hortense gave Sidonia a subtle hint that Charles II's capacious heart had no room for her that summer. So she returned to France, no doubt to find another lover. Hortense and Sidonia had one thing in common, an awareness of their beauty.

During February 1677 Hortense appeared in a very conspicuous position raised above all the other ladies behind the throne, so that nobody any longer doubted her ascendancy at Court.[9] If any further evidence were needed that she was Chanticleer's *maitresse en titre*, she now received a pension of £4,100 from him. On hearing of this her husband tried to argue that the money was really owing to the Mazarin estate by Charles, who had borrowed a considerable amount of money from Cardinal Mazarin during his exile. When Armand Mazarin warned Charles that Hortense's receipts were invalid, the King merely smiled, saying that he did not bother about receipts from ladies anyway. Then the Duc Mazarin obtained an audience with King Louis and managed to procure his permission to withhold paying the pension for a while.

If Hortense had been politically ambitious, like the Duchess of Portsmouth, she might have maintained her position for quite a long time, but her volatile, mercurial temperament was her undoing. She held all the cards in her favour, but she just didn't care. Her admirer the Prince of Monaco, who lived in his castle on the rock overlooking Monte Carlo, was desperately in love with her during the winter 1676-1677. At first she gave him little hope that she would succumb to his pleading, but was far from indifferent to him.

Courtin wrote to Louvois (January 21st 1677): "Monsieur de Monaco is the most in love of all men, but his profound melancholy makes me doubtful whether his love will be successful." The Ambassador was wrong. By July the Prince's impatience could brook no further denial as his health was affected by the English climate. His pleading that she should yield herself to him now became even more urgent since he was suffering from tertiary fever and a heart disease, and wished to return to his castle. She gave way at last and agreed to sleep with him, despite St. Evrémond's

82

remonstrances that she must use more discretion. How could she afford to live in comfort if she cuckolded the King on whom she largely depended? Her anxious friends warned her that Charles would cease to pay her the £4,000 if her affair with the Prince of Monaco continued. It was soon the talk of the town. Hortense then was candid enough to admit to her regal lover that he would be foolish to count on her fidelity to him any longer. After hesitating a while Charles angrily revoked her pension, but he soon restored it.[10] It was not in the nature of this amiable monarch to harbour resentment for long. He had once written his best loved sister Henriette Duchesse d'Orléans that he was ever indulgent to frailties of this kind. Although he retained a fondness for Hortense, he never really loved her, taking pleasure in her society and thinking how beautiful she looked as she recited passages from Racine or the poetry of La Fontaine. He appreciated, too, that she listened to his stories, seldom interrupting. Possessing a lot of Latin blood through his late mother Henrietta Maria's maternal family, he understood her moods, her selfishness, the sudden flood of tears and the passion, alternating with the calm moments of reflection and blissful idleness.

Such a woman clinging to her liberty above all else, obeying no conventional code, wanting constant change and variety in her life rather than permanent ties, is bound to make a disastrous marriage. So far also none of her many lovers, including Couberville, Saint-Réal, Charles II and the Prince of Monaco had touched her very deeply. She was only to experience great love once in her extraordinary life, resulting in tragedy because of her fatal attraction for all sorts of men, members of the female sex and even close relations.

CHAPTER VIII

Hortense and St. Evrémond

Today we are too apt to think of the gaiety at the Court of the Second Charles, and to forget the dark clouds that obscured the horizon in 1678. This was the year when Titus Oates, a despicable rogue, made his mendacious accusations against many innocent people, the year of the Popish plot. Oates accused the Duchesse Mazarin as a Popish whore and a French agent, but few Catholics, however innocent, escaped his slander. Hortense enjoyed the friendship of many protestants, including Charles II's natural son by Lucy Walter, James Duke of Monmouth. Much was made of an alleged remark of Hortense's that it would be very easy to kill the King, but a Roman Catholic priest named Father Oliva, stated quite correctly that the Duchesse Mazarin was more interested in enjoying herself than concerning herself seriously in matters political or religious.[1] What possible reason could the lady have for killing the King? In this age of bitter satires and lampoons it would be surprizing if sordid attacks were not made on her immorality. A typical example is *Rochester's Farewell to Court 1680*, and it is unfortunate that a lyrical poet of surpassing genius should descend to such depths.

Hortense lost all her political importance in England after 1677. Honoré de Courtin was succeeded by Paul Barillon as French ambassador during August, but he rarely alludes to her in his Despatches and the Duchesse Mazarin is not even mentioned in his 'Instructions'. True, one despatch written on February 9th 1682 refers to King Charles attempting to regain for her the pension which her husband had ceased to pay her.[2] Barillon was extremely astute, but a much less agreeable personality than Courtin, more suited to deal with bribery and corruption in high places. For the remainder of Charles II's reign, the Duchess of Portsmouth's supremacy at Court was never again seriously challenged.

The extraordinary friendship which grew up between Hortense and St. Evrémond puzzled their contemporaries, for he was over thirty years older than her, having been born in 1613. Despite his age, St. Evrémond was passionately attached to the Duchesse Mazarin, the most constant of her many admirers. Hence his sadness when he admits to her that he would have liked to be her lover:[3]

> 'J'ai voulu devenir Amant
> On me veut Ami seulement:
> Ami traité d'une manière;
> Quelquefois douce et familière;
> Mais indignement rebuté
> S'il prend la moindre liberté.'

Yet being a realist, he would write to her with a subtle irony, his letter tinged with humour as if laughing at himself:

> "How unfortunate is my condition . . . should I ask you to love a person of my age? I have not lived in a manner to expect a miracle in my favour."

If the sincerity of his merits received an acknowledgment from her that she regretted that he was old and a wish that he was young, he would be content. "The favour of a wish is a small thing indeed, do not refuse me . . ." "There was never a passion so disinterested as mine." Indeed he regarded her lovers as her subjects, instead of hating them as his rivals.[4] He established himself as a sort of indispensable Secretary of State.

The Duchesse Mazarin may be described as the main inspiration in St. Evrémond's literary life. Not only did he address a prolific amount of work, both in prose and verse to her, such as his *Defence* of some plays of M. Corneille, his *Reflections* on the French, Spanish, Italian and English Comedies and on operas, but he composed most of her important letters, especially those relating to her husband.[5] His correspondence is most curious, throwing light on the characters of many of their mutual friends: Ralph Lord Montagu, a magnificent builder, the Duke of Buckingham, Edmund Waller described by Aubrey as above middle height and of a dark complexion, and Charles Lord Buckhurst (now Earl of

Dorset), a former lover of Nell Gwyn. Their real value is their beauty and originality. They succeed in recreating the seventeenth century society in which he moved and the age in which he lived. However, St. Evrémond has his critics, among them Armand Jean du Plessis, Duc de Richelieu, who dubbed him "a half-scholar who knows too much for weak intelligences, too little for strong . . . rash and daring."[6] Dryden, a very fine critic, thought highly of St. Evrémond, writing in 1692:

> "There is not only a justness in his conceptions, which is the foundation of good writing, but also a purity of language and a beautiful turn of words so little understood by modern writers."

Another French critic, the Duc d'Aumale "thought his prose, not his verse, exquisite and delicate".

Hortense was fond enough of St. Evrémond in her selfish way, but she made use of him when she needed money or clothes, although he could ill afford to give her any out of his meagre purse. Nowhere is she more alive than in his letters and odes. Occasionally St. Evrémond revolted against some imagined cruelty or real unkindness, but his craving for affection made him overlook her outbursts of passion, her reckless extravagance and her almost pathological liking for cleanliness. She could hardly tolerate the untidyness of the poet when she visited him in his lodgings, while her passion for fresh air exasperated St. Evrémond. It seems to be more characteristic of our own age than the later seventeenth century. He constantly complained that her house was draughty. How well St. Evrémond understood her finest qualities, her tremendous courage, her need to live dangerously. "Do not fear anything so much," he conjured her in his verse, "as the calm of the waves, it needs a great storm; you hate the sea without peril of shipwreck."

His *bête noir* was the French croupier Morin, who after fleeing from France, found refuge in London; an unpleasant character, insinuating and knavish, who introduced basset into England. St. Evrémond strongly disapproved of the Duchesse's increasing addiction for gambling, mainly because he feared her health suffered

Cardinal Jules Mazarin 1602-1661 by Pierre Mignard; Louis XIV's great mini-ster during his adolescence.

Hortense Mancini Duchesse Mazarin from an engraving by G. Valote after the picture by Sir Peter Lely.

Meeting of Louis XIV and Philip IV June 6th 1660 concerning the betrothal of Marie Thérèse. Gobelin tapestry after Charles Lebrun (Versailles).

Olympe Mancini 1640-1708.

Louis XIV. Miniature by Petitot at Montague House.

Hortense Mancini Duchesse Mazarin by Pierre Mignard, a leading artist at the Court of Louis XIV who particularly excelled in painting women.

Cardinal Jules Mazarin 1602-1661. Eng. Nanteuil after Claveau.

St. James's Palace and part of the City of Westminster 1660.

CITY of WESTMINSTER.

N.th side of Pall Mall

about the Year 1660.

of John Towneley, of Towneley, Esq. T.B.M. F.R.S. R.A.

*Marianne Mancini Duchesse de Bouillon, the youngest of the Mancini sisters,
a patron of poets. Print in the Bibliothèque Naitonale, Paris.*

Olympe Mancini Comtesse de Soissons. Olympe's husband, Prince Eugène de Savoie-Carignan, treated as being of the blood royal. From a contemporary print.

Hortense Mancini telling her sister's fortune.

Ralph First Duke of Montagu 1638-1709, a devotee of French architecture, by J. Closterman.

Duchesse Hortense Mazarin by Sir Godfrey Kneller.

Charles II after P. Lely.

Charles Marguetel Seigneur de Saint Evrémond c. 1701 by James Parmentier.

during the feverish nocturnal hours playing basset. "Beaux yeux, quel est votre destin!" he wrote peevishly. "Périrez-vous, beaux yeux, à regarder Morin." It annoyed him that Hortense's erudite friends such as Vossius and Justel were no longer welcome guests.

After her nocturnal gambling at Newmarket much frequented by Charles II during the spring and autumn for the horse matches, Hortense liked to gallop on horseback on Newmarket Downs. "Do not fear, Madame, to lose your charms at Newmarket."[7]

Cock fighting was then much in vogue, and Hortense would attend this spectacle, seeming to approve of it. St. Evrémond conjured her: "Cry louder than my Lord Thomond" (an Irish peer Henry O'Brian organiser of cock fights). Charles Cotton described this brutal sport as one "full of delight and pleasure", but Pepys considered it barbaric after he had attended a cock fight in Shoe Lane. Always fond of the theatre, Hortense would attend performances of Shakespeare's *Henry VIII* or Thomas Heywood's *Queen Elizabeth*. "Eat oysters at supper," wrote her philosopher wit,

> "and pass the entire night without sleeping; your beauty which has escaped Monsieur Morin's basset, will survive indeed the fatigues of Newmarket."[8]

Hortense liked to collect rare objects and curiosities. For that purpose she would go down to the docks on the Thames, to board the vessels arriving from the East, and buy the most expensive and rarest articles displayed there. She took infinite trouble in her dress, for she possessed excellent taste. She excelled both Marie and Olympe in her dress sense. Marianne on the other hand so essentially feminine, was not in the least interested in fashions. According to Saint-Simon no woman occupied herself less in her toilet.[9]

Hortense spared no extravagance buying lace from Venice, horn combs from Italy, gloves, fans and other articles from abroad.[10] With her exquisite Italianate beauty she looked radiant in a black flowered satin gown bordered with embroidered lace she ordered from France.

Charles II occasionally had her as a mistress, but their relations were now mainly friendly. Occasionally he interfered, forbidding Ralph Montagu to visit her about 1680, probably fearing that this incessant intriguer was again trying to involve her in his political machinations. Anne Digby Countess of Sunderland wrote to her lover Henry Sydney, March 22nd:

> "Mr. Montagu goes no more to Madam Mazarin's, the town says he is forbid; whether his love or his politics were too pressing I know not."[11]

It is not likely that Charles worried whether Hortense was indulging in a liaison with Ralph Montagu or not.

The Duchesse Mazarin, like all the Mancinis, loved animals and her house was full of dogs, cats and every species of bird. Her uncle the Cardinal had been attached to his monkeys and Hortense shared his taste. St. Evrémond, knowing of her fondness for birds, gave her a white sparrow that "whistled for eight shillings". He told her that it played a thousand pretty tricks, which was unusual for sparrows. As her extensive aviary contained bullfinches, goldfinches, a parrot, a nightingale and a starling named Jacob, and she also owned many cats, one can but hope that the latter did not inflict too much danger on her birds. We know the names of her dogs: "Boy", "Little Rogue" and "Chop".

When Hortense was away from London, possibly at Bath, Newmarket or Windsor, St. Evrémond was commissioned to visit her house and to report that all was well with her animals. It must have resembled a miniature zoo. He wrote her:

> "Pretty (her parrot) is quite well, he is a well born bird . . . My first visit is made to Pretty, my second to the chickens, which are the worthiest (les plus honnêtes) chickens I have seen in my life. They prefer an old cock covered with scars, an old wounded soldier, who could well demand a place among the pensioners at Newmarket. They prefer him to a young gallant, who has the finest coat and the finest tail in the world. I must fain be content with my condition, such as it is, but if I had to choose I would rather be a cock among these virtuous hens than an old man among these ladies."[12]

St. Evrémond's wonderful description of the Duchesse's cock "strutting with an extraordinary gravity, glorying in the respect paid him" must have richly amused her.

Oddly enough he disapproved of her going to Bath to drink the waters, maintaining that they were harmful to her health. "If you are in a reasonably good state of health," he admonished her, "do not either take a bath, nor the waters; the best waters are often harmful to those who are well and rarely do well to those who are sick."[13] She liked to take her page Dery with her because he had a beautiful voice. "Make Monsieur Dery sing and Monsieur Milon (her confessor) preach," St. Evrémond would tell her. Dery was later very upset when he realized his voice was breaking. He wanted to be castrated. Fortunately St. Evrémond persuaded him against such a drastic step. He gave a nickname to Hortense's rather solemn English valet Stourton, calling him "The Young Senator". Occasionally St. Evrémond used him as a messenger to send Hortense books. Stourton was jealous of Dery, so admired by the ladies for his lovely voice.

Her chef Galet had a European reputation for his magnificent cuisine, and she took infinite trouble to send to Paris for choice delicacies unobtainable in England. Small wonder if visitors took advantage of her generosity and extravagance to flock to her table. Her wines were carefully chosen by St. Evrémond, especially partial to champagne, though he did not care for burgundy. He often depended on his great friend Ninon de Lenclos to procure for him the best vintages.[14] On one occasion when the Duchesse was absent at Bath, St. Evrémond playfully chided her:

"It was enough, Madam to deprive me of your hospitality by your journey to take the waters, you only needed to take away Galet, and to make me unable to eat at my own expense. I have lost everything in losing Galet."

While she was away St. Evrémond and Mylord Montagu, the eminent Protestant refugee M. Justel and M. Silvestre to dine with him. He wrote:

"Mylord Montagu faithful to mutton, had difficulty in

stomaching veal, but when he had eaten it and I had told him that it came from you, he swore not to eat mutton in his life unless you were kind enough to send it from Bath."

By way of return for her generous hospitality to him, St. Evrémond would sometimes send her charming gifts of flowers and fruit. He wrote her:

"As all the world gives you fruit, I will not be the only person who gives you none. Receive peaches from a man who has no garden, with as good a heart as he gives you them. I ought not to have made use of the word Heart: that word ought no more to come out of the mouth of a man at my age than that of Health. But without Heart, and without Health, I am hasta la muerte."[15]

Sometimes he would jocularly sign his letters "Le Chevalier de la Triste Figure" and he occasionally prevailed upon her to subscribe herself Dulcinee.

Besides Mustapha, the Duchesse Mazarin's faithful little Moor, first given to her by the Duke of Savoy, there now served her a negro nicknamed Pompey. Dery and Stourton were her pages, while two waiting-women, one French and another Spanish, co-served her in this capacity. Her household was fairly large, certainly far above her means.

One day when Hortense was suffering from one of her occasional fits of depression, she expressed a wish to know what people would say of her after her death. So St. Evrémond in his witty fashion, hastened to oblige her by composing his "Funeral Oration of the Duchesse Mazarin". "What country is there that Madame Mazarin has not seen; what country visited by her has not admired her?" Then by way of blandishment he writes:

"This Rome at all times so glorious, is more vain to have given her to the world than of having produced all her heroes."[16]

Her lodgings in her house in St. James's, vulgarly known as

"Le Petit Palais", were not only the haunt of erudite men, but frequented by courtiers. Two of her closest friends were Louis de Duras Earl of Feversham, a naturalized Frenchman and a great dandy. Feversham was Master of the Horse and Lord Chamberlain to Catherine of Braganza, Charles II's Portuguese Queen. Although a nephew of the great Turenne, he showed meagre ability as a soldier, and was later accused of indolence at the Battle of Sedgemoor (1685) when commanding James II's forces against the Duke of Monmouth. Fortunately John Lord Churchill, the future Duke of Marlborough, showed his mettle, proving him a very efficient second-in-command. Henri de Massau de Ruvigni, a son of the Marquis de Ruvigni, a former French ambassador in London, was an eminent soldier. However, while later serving in Ireland, he displeased St. Evrémond by sending Hortense liberal quantities of whisky (usquebaos), for he was certain that her partiality for strong spirits and white wine would injure her health.

John Evelyn later in his Diary (June 11th 1699) describes the Duchesse Mazarin as "an extraordinary beauty and wit, but dissolute and impatient of matrimonial restraint."

One of her most intimate women friends was Charlotte Beverweert, a Lady of the Bedchamber to Princess Anne (later Queen). She seems to have acted as a sort of housekeeper for Hortense, relieving her of many chores. St. Evrémond, who was always leaping into verse, makes Charlotte a lively character in a Dialogue between the three friends. When Madame Mazarin's friend, the beautiful Jane Middleton died - she had broken many hearts - St. Evrémond commemorated her.

During the summer (1683) Hortense experienced a great sorrow, a desolating tragedy that would affect the remainder of her life. In her thirty-seventh year she was very much in love with a Swedish nobleman Baron de Banier, a son of a famous general. After arriving in London, having been presented to Hortense, he very soon became her lover. Hortense's emotions were now deeply involved where in her numerous other affairs of the heart they for the most part had only touched the surface. Unfortunately Philippe de Soissons, youngest son of her sister Olympe, came to London about this time and fell passionately in love with his endearing aunt.[17] Realizing that he had a deadly rival in the Baron de Banier, the jealous young man stung to madness, challenged the Swede to a duel and wounded him so desperately that he died a few days later. The tragedy at least shows the power of Hortense's attraction, for she had lost none of her celebrated beauty.

Hortense was absolutely grief-stricken, not only by her lover's death, but troubled about her nephew Philippe. He had offended against the duelling-edicts. After being prosecuted and punished, he was smuggled out of the country when the scandal had died down and the Swedish government had been appeased. For a time Hortense had her apartments hung with black and refused to receive visitors, even her most intimate friends.

Madame de Sévigné, fascinated as always by the Mancinis, wrote to her daughter: "One would not have thought that the eyes of a grandmother could have done such execution."[18]

How curious to think of the lovely Hortense as a grandmother, but we must recall that during those earlier six years of her marriage she had given her husband three daughters, Marie Charlotte born in 1662, Marie Anne in 1663, Marie Olympe in 1665 and Paul Jules her only son born in 1667. It is likely that Madame de Sévigné was referring to Marie Olympe, who married the Marquis de Bellefonds and had a child by him by 1683. It is unlikely that Hortense's children counted much in her life, for her maternal instincts were hardly very strong. The calm pleasures of domesticity were not for the tempestuous Hortense. She was herself too much of a child, made to be loved and admired.

In her grief Hortense even thought seriously of retiring to a convent, much to the dismay of St. Evrémond, who knew her so well and how completely unsuited she would be as an inmate. He waited for a while, then wrote her:

> "Since the unfortunate evening when you apprized me of the extremely sad decision that you wish to take, I have not had a moment's rest or to express it better, you have left me an incessant pain . . . How is it possible for you to leave persons who are charmed with you, and who adore you: friends who love you better than they love themselves, to go and hunt after unknown people you do not like, and who, perhaps, will insult you? Do you consider, Madam, that you are go-

ing to throw yourself into a convent, which the Constable's Lady, your sister (Marie) abhorred? . . . What will you find, Madam, in a nunnery? A severe prohibition of all that nature reasonably requires, of all that humanity allows. A cell, a hard bed, more detestable diet, nasty stinking clothes . . . You will be your sole attendant, the only person to humour and please you amidst so many things that will displease you."[19]

He told her that her wonderful beauty, this great ornament of the universe, was not bestow'd upon her to be hid.

"You owe yourself to the public, to your friends, to yourself. You were made to please yourself, to please all, to dissipate sadness, to inspire joy, and to revive in general all that languishes . . . I do not doubt at all that you hope to find much comfort in My Lady Colonna's conversation, but if I am not mistaken that comfort will not last long. After you have talked three or four days of France and Italy, of the passion of the King (Louis) and the timidity of the Cardinal, of what you are like to be and what you are at present . . ."

In such a way did St. Evrémond use powerful argument to banish from her mind such a desperate recourse.

"When ugly and stupid women throw themselves into convents, it is divine inspiration which makes them leave the world where they only appear to put their creator to shame. In your case, Madam, it is a true temptation of the devil, who envious of God's glory, cannot bear the admiration which his finest work gives."

It seemed to him that Hortense grieved too much over the death of her lover.

"It is a most unfortunate affair," he told her,

"but there is nothing extraordinary in this adventure except your grief. Lovers are mortal like other men. Your lover is now no more than a sad and empty shell formed by your imagination."

Perhaps St. Evrémond did not sufficiently take into account the depth of Hortense's love for the handsome young diplomat. It is easy to be philosophical when one's life is pursuing an even tenor. When Hortense experienced real difficulties she gave way too readily to despair, resigning herself to those whose only interest was her ruin.

Hearing of her intention to enter a convent, Armand Mazarin in a fit of religious zeal and lacking any understanding of his wife's mentality, sent Madame de Ruz to London, instructing her to do everything possible to persuade Hortense to take this step. This was the same French lady whom her husband during their early marriage had set to spy on her. Hortense and Madame de Ruz wept together, and in her weakened state, the older lady strongly urged Hortense to take the vows. St. Evrémond detested Madame de Ruz, thinking quite rightly that she had a depressing influence on the Duchesse Mazarin. He begged Hortense to get rid of her, and she was returned to France. Eventually her zest for life and the society of her many friends changed her sentiments. No longer did she retain any desire to retire to a convent.

Henceforward, however, she was never quite so gay as formerly. Her temper became more unpredictable, subject to bouts of marked irritability. She accused St. Evrémond of speaking against her to their many friends, an unjust suspicion absolutely devoid of truth, said the old man. "You are cruel," he retorted, "I never spoke ill of you." Why should she turn on him so unfairly? "Bring back those happy times," he would urge. Her moods were partly caused by her liking for and her too free indulgence in wine and spirits. There were quarrels and sweet reconciliations. When harmony prevailed he would teaze her about her latest conquest, Mylord Godolphin.

Sidney Godolphin, a Cornishman, had started his career as a page to Charles II and the King was later to say of him when he became head of the Treasury: "He was never in the way, and never out of it." According to Bishop Burnet "he was the silentest and modestest man that was ever lived in a Court." Although an exclusionist, having voted for the exclusion of the Duke of York from the throne (1681), he became much attached to James's Duchess Mary of Modena after being appointed her Chamberlain and it is likely that he admired Hortense in much the same way, a sort of platonic love, as he did the Duchess of York.

When we consider womens' involvement in public life today, for example our first female Prime Minister Margaret Thatcher, it is curious to get St. Evrémond's opinion in 1678. "I have wondered," he wrote,

> "a hundred times why the Fair sex had been excluded from the management of publick affairs, for I found some of them more skilful and abler than men. I was at length, sensible that this exclusion did not proceed either from the malice of envy, or any suggestion of private interest . . . A woman who may wisely govern a kingdom one day, will give herself a master the next, as one would not entrust with the looking after a dozen of hens, to use Cardinal Mazarin's own words."

He cited Lucy Percy Countess of Carlisle, the intimate friend of Queen Henrietta Maria, Madame de Chevreuse, a great friend of Anne of Austria and the Princess Palantine Anne de Gonzague as three ambitious women, who liked to dominate others.

The winter of the great frost preceding the death of Charles II (February 1685) was so severe that even the Thames was frozen over. John Evelyn's celebrated account of the scene in Whitehall on Charles II's last night before his illness, toying with his mistresses, Hortense Mazarin, Louise Duchess of Portsmouth and Barbara Duchess of Cleveland, is too well known to require much comment. The diarist was shocked, but all three ladies were by now favourite companions rather than lovers. Charles never discarded his mistresses, he merely added to them. To the murmur of the animated chatter, a French boy (I am tempted to say that this was Dery, Hortense's page, but Dery was English) with a lovely voice sang love songs,

> "in that glorious gallery while some twenty dissolute courtiers

played at basset at an adjoining table, and the chink of gold, £2,000 sounded oddly in the night air."

It was a Sunday. "Six days after was all in the dust," Evelyn wrote.

Although Hortense had never loved Charles, she was sincerely attached to him and extremely grieved by his death. St. Evrémond thought that her grief was excessive. "He was just another lover," he told her, but Hortense was inconsolable. It was fortunate for her that the new Queen Mary of Modena was her Martinozzi cousin, and James II, influenced by his wife, continued the Duchesse Mazarin's pension.

CHAPTER IX

Olympe's Downfall

Olympe Comtesse de Soissons, 'Madame La Comtesse' as she was known at Louix XIV's Court, was deprived of her important post of Superintendent of the Queen's household during March 1679. This was not intended as a disgrace, for the King told her that she had given Queen Marie Thérèse every satisfaction and she agreed to accept 200,000 écus (petits écus of 3 livres) as a parting gift. Louis wanted the post for Madame de Montespan, who had hankered after it for many years. It was his way of showing the arrogant favourite, so insatiable in bed, that she was no longer his mistress. A new beauty, Mlle. de Fontangues, had appeared at Court from Auvergne, only eighteen years of age, foolish and provincial, but as fresh as a ripe peach. Her parents instructed her to become King Louis's mistress, and Angélique de Fontangues was nothing loath. Louis doted on her, but after suffering a miscarriage Angélique had the misfortune of losing a great deal of blood. Mme de Sévigné called it "being wounded in the King's service". When she died, many people suspected the hand of her jealous rival Mme. de Montespan.

Olympe's downfall was owing to her dabbling in Black Magic, her Mancini attraction for sorcery and the occult. The greatest scandal of the Sun King's glorious reign burst on his Court like a clap of thunder. Towards the end of 1678 Gabriel Nicolas de la Reynie, Lieutenant of Police, got wind of a supposed plot to poison King Louis and the Dauphin. After closely inquiring into the affair, several of the more prominent sorceresses, including Marie Bosse and a woman named La Vigoureux, were arrested, followed by the arrest during March 1679 of the most notorious of them all, the sorceress known as La Voisin. Her real name was Catherine Monvoisin (née Deshayes), one of the most evil and depraved criminals in history. When Olympe heard of La Voisin's apprehension she was most uneasy, fearful what the woman would confess. Together with her sister Marianne Duchesse de Bouillon, she had been among her many fashionable clients. La Voisin had been born in Paris and from an early age possessed an uncanny gift for reading character in the face and divining the secret thoughts of others. "Since the age of nine," she said, "I have studied necromancy and physiognomy."

Ladies fearing to lose their lovers bought her love-powders. La Voisin made what was considered in that age a large income from her profession, ten thousand francs per annum. When she received her clients she would be splendidly dressed in a sea-green velvet robe decorated with French-point-lace, her shoes woven from silver thread and embroidered with eagles of fine gold. Married to a haberdasher with a shop on the Pont de Sainte-Marie, she had many titled lovers as well as the headsman of Paris.

After La Reynie had announced the results of his investigations, King Louis, absolutely horrified, decided on the advice of his minster Louvois to set up a tribunal called the Royal Chamber of the Arsenal, more popularly known as the Chambre Ardente, 'the burning chamber', for the trial of accused persons. Nobody was immune from prosecution, the common people, the Bourgeoiserie (the Middle Class) or the nobility. "Impieties, sacrilege and abominations are virtually commonplace in and around Paris and in the provinces" La Reynie had discovered.

The case against Olympe mainly rested on the evidence of La Voisin, who not only accused her of having her husband poisoned, but of indulging in threats against King Louis and his earlier mistress Louise de la Vallière. M. Funck-Brentano in his fascinating work *Le Drame des Poisons* maintained that all La Voisin's disclosures were found to be accurate.

Olympe, together with two other ladies, visited the sorceress only on one occasion, almost certainly in the early 1660's. Louis was at this period very enamoured of Louise de la Vallière, and the Comtesse de Soissons blamed her for the King's changed feelings, his antipathy for her. When giving Olympe a hand reading in her garden, La Voisin told her that she did not know the identity of her client until later - that she had been loved by a great prince. When she eagerly demanded whether this love would return, La Voisin's answer was very guarded. According to her evidence, the

Comtesse de Soissons spoke of finding means to avenge her wrongs. When questioned later (January 16th 1680) by La Reynie and two Commissioners, the sorceress stated that Olympe had told her "that she would destroy both the King and La Vallière." This was damning enough, but there is no indication whatsoever that she made a definite attempt to effect this design.

The publicity ruined Olympe's career at Court. Aware that her powerful enemies, including Madame de Montespan, not yet implicated in l'affaire des poisons, and Louvois, a friend of the favourite, were influencing the King against her, Olympe sought refuge in flight rather than face trial in the Chambre Ardente. In this resolve she was undoubtedly encouraged by Louis, activated by a natural dread that his own dignity would be compromised if embarrassing and intimate matters were disclosed in Court. He had been fond of Olympe, a former mistress, but he knew her character too well and that her vindictive spirit would not spare him if she found it necessary.

Madame de Sévigné relates many picturesque details about the sordid L'Affaire des Poisons. She wrote to her daughter (January 26th 1680):

> "As for the Comtesse de Soissons, she could not endure the thought of a prison, they were willing to allow her time to make her escape, if she really were guilty."

Louis ordered her brother-in-law, the Duc de Bouillon, Marianne's husband, to go round to the Hôtel de Soissons, where Olympe was playing at basset on a Wednesday with some friends - she was always a great gambler.

There he begged her to step into a closet where he gave her the King's message. There were two choices. She must either leave France or go to the Bastille. Olympe was not prepared to face the music. She hurriedly ordered her servants to pack some cases and after visiting her mother-in-law, the Princesse de Carignan, left Paris in tears at 3 a.m. telling her people that she was innocent, but the vile woman La Voisin and her associates had taken pleasure in denouncing her. Louvois wrote to the President of the Chambre Ardente that the King had sent two officers of his guard to arrest

Madame La Comtesse and her friend the Marquise d'Alluye. However, it was merely a feint. The last thing Louis wanted was for her to stand her trial.

Having crossed the Flemish border, the Comtesse de Soissons wrote to Louis, saying she was willing to return to appear before the Chambre Ardente, provided she was not subjected to the ordeal and indignity of imprisonment in the Bastille or Vincennes before her trial. Louis made no reply to her appeal.

Olympe continued her journey to Brussels, then the capital of the Spanish Netherlands, having to suffer many indignities from the mob. The gates of Namur and Antwerp were closed to her, the people pestering her crying: "We want no poisoners here." "Henceforward in foreign countries a Frenchman and a poisoner will be the same thing."[1] Their insults reveal at least how insular people were in that epoch. At Brussels a powerful protector, the Comte de Monterey, took her under his wing, but she had to endure many afflictions.

Madame de Sévigné, who heard the story from the Duc de la Rochefoucauld (the son of the celebrated author of *The Maximes*) related "that the Comtesse upon entering a Brussels church had been forced to steal out of it, for some people had contrived a sort of dance of a number of cats tied together, or rather out of mere malice raised so horrible a caterwauling and squeaking, crying at the same time that they were a parcel of devils and witches that followed her, that she was obliged as I said, to quit the place and to give way to this piece of folly." Another example revealing the primitive superstition then prevailing.

She was now aged forty, still very attractive, but unhappy unless she was the centre of attention. A little court gradually formed round her, including a great admirer, the Prince of Parma, who had succeeded de Monterey as governor. She continued her wandering life. After eight years we find her living in Madrid deeply involved in sordid political intrigues.

Marianne Duchesse de Bouillon, almost as deeply involved in L'Affaire des Poisons as her elder sister, showed more intelligence and dexterity in extricating herself from her worse troubles. According to the Marchioness de Sévigné writing to her daughter from Paris (January 31st 1680):

"The Duchesse de Bouillon went to ask La Voison for a small dose of the poison to kill an old tiresome husband she had with a nostrum to marry a young man (Monsieur de Vendôme) she was fond of."

Two of La Voisin's chief accomplices, a man named Lesage (his real name was Adam Coeuret) and a sorceress La Vigoureux, both gave deadly evidence against her in their earlier examinations. Lesage, a former wool merchant, stated that he had met her at La Voisin's house where she had demanded the death of the Duc de Bouillon and the means to marry the Duc de Vendôme. Lesage was a charlatan, though possessing remarkable ability as a juggler. Consequently one cannot rely on his evidence. He told the Commissioners that the Duchesse de Bouillon only applied to him to use his magic powers after other means had failed. The Witch La Vigoureux had informed Lesage that the lady had visited him for the same purpose, but the dose of poison supplied had no effect. How fortunate for Marianne that La Vigoureux died under torture before her summons to appear before the Chambre Ardente. This encouraged her to adopt a disdainful, haughty attitude towards her judges, for La Vigoureux would have been the principal witness against her.

When Marianne appeared before the Chambre Ardente, she arrived in a coach drawn by six horses, seated between her husband and her lover Monsieur de Vendôme. Followed by twenty more coaches in which were seated many of her friends and sympathizers, the smartest and best dressed gentlemen and ladies of the Court. Saint-Simon mentions the Duchesse de Bouillon entering the Chambre Ardente like "une petite reine".[2] She answered La Reynie's questions with an air of injured innocence. Despite her bold appearance and her arrogance, Marianne was in considerable danger. When she confronted the Court she insisted that she only came there out of respect for King Louis, since she did not recognize the Chambre Ardente. As a Duchesse she had the right to be tried by all the assembled Chambers of Parliament. So she refused to answer the President of the Court's questions until this had been recorded.

She removed her gloves, taking care to display her beautiful hands. Facing her accusers, she possessed much of the intelligence of her late uncle the Cardinal. Funck-Brentano in *Le Drame des Poisons* relates her skill in parrying their menace.

> "Did you know La Vigoureux?"
> "No."
> "Do you know La Voisin?"
> "Yes."
> "Why did you want to do away with your husband?"

Marianne looked at her judges, almost seeming to enjoy herself, and arching her eyes in their startled innocence exclaimed:

> "I do away with my husband! Why, you have only to ask him if he thinks so! He gave me his hand to this very door."
> "But why did you go so often to La Voisin's house?"
> "I wanted to see the Sibyls and prophetesses she promised to show me. Such a company would have been well worth all my journeys."[3]

Eventually Marianne asked in her mocking way: "Well, Messieurs, is that all you have to say to me?"

"Yes, Madame," they replied. Whereupon the Duchesse de Bouillon exclaimed by no means *sotta voce* as she left the Court, "Really, I should never have believed that men of sense could ask so many foolish questions." During the proceedings she was examined very closely as to her dealings with Lesage.

Voltaire writing in the eighteenth century mentions the Duchesse de Bouillon's quick wit in replying to La Reynie when he asked her: "Did you ever see the devil at La Voisin's house, since you went there to meet him?" "Monsieur," she replied, "I see him here at this very moment. He is ugly and old and disguised as a Judge."[4]

It was foolish of Marianne to boast too openly of her skill in Court, for the King heard of it and she was given a lettre de cachet banishing her to Nérac at the foot of the Pyrenees.[5] Madame de Sévigné wrote to her daughter (February 14th 1680): "Madame de Bouillon has gloried in the answers she made the judges . . . She set out yesterday in great affliction." During August 1682 she was given permission to return to Court. Three years later she was again in disgrace and exiled to Evreux.

One inclines to the view that there is strong doubt as to whether she was innocent: "If she be innocent," wrote Madame de Sévigné,

"she is a great loser in being refused the pleasure of triumphing; if guilty she is happy in shunning the infamy of being confronted and possibly convicted . . . Let us consider the four sisters and what a wandering planet governs their fates! One (Marie Colonna) sent into Spain, another into England (Hortense Mazarin), a third into Flanders (Olympe de Soissons) and a fourth (Marianne de Bouillon) into the remotest parts of Guienne . . ."

It was later discovered that Athenais de Montespan was herself deeply implicated in L'Affaire des Poisons. Never over confident in Louis's fidelity and dreading the loss of his love, the royal favourite had dabbled pretty freely in black magic. It is certain that she visited the foul sorceress La Voisin from 1666 onwards. She supplied Athenais with various concoctions and powders such as excrement and toad's spittle designed to quicken or stimulate a fading love.[6] Her eleven year reign as royal mistress was finally terminated, despite the attempts of Louvois to save her. What hurt Louis most and he was very vulnerable, were the criminal activities of people implicated in these nefarious transactions, for they harmed his image in the eyes of foreigners as well as his own subjects, sullying what he loved most, his *gloire*.

As for La Voisin, she met her deserts (February 1680).

"Despite being put to the torture . . . she gave loose to her debauched behaviour, to the scandal of every one present . . they tried to make her sensible of the badness of her conduct, and that it would be better to employ her time in thinking of God, and singing some pious hymns than those loose and idle songs, . . . She came from Vincennes to Paris in a coach. At five o'clock (in the evening) she was bound to set on the sledge dressed in white, with a taper in her hand

> . . . and at Greve she struggled with all her might to prevent them taking her out of the sledge . . . She was bound by iron chains and then covered over with straw; she swore prodigiously and pushed away the straw five or six times. . . . She gave her soul to the devil very prettily in the middle of the flames; indeed she only went from one fire to another."[7]

While her sisters pursued their chequered lives in France and the Spanish Netherlands, Marie was living in the Convent of San Domingo-el-Real in Madrid. When her husband Prince Colonna arrived during early November 1678, Marie was greatly alarmed fearing he intended to carry her off against her will to Italy with the help of a ruffian named Francesco Restá, a fugitive from Rome to Spain to escape his crimes. She dreaded lest he might assassinate her on the journey. So Marie resolutely refused to leave Madrid.

When the young, attractive Queen Maria Luisa, elder daughter of Monsieur (Louis XIV's younger brother) made her magnificent entry into Madrid on January 13th 1680 - she had recently married Carlos II of Spain, Carlos the bewitched (hechizado) as he is called, Marie thought that she would acquire a powerful ally and friend in the French-born Queen. Monsieur always had a soft spot for his childhood friend. Since she wished to see the entry of the Queen of Spain, Marie asked her husband's permission to stay for a few days at the house of his brother-in-law the Marques de Los Balbases, forgetful, perhaps, that Balbases harboured a grudge for an alleged insult when she had first come to Italy. To her surprise Colonna immediately granted her his permission.

As she watched from a balcony Maria Luisa riding her Andalusian horse with superb skill, looking extremely pretty, dressed in her little farthingale and low-cut bodice and wearing in her plumed hat an enormous pearl called Pellegrina and on her finger the King's superb diamond, Marie felt an overwhelming sadness, a deadness of the spirit. Her mind was carried back to that other occasion twenty years ago when she watched the entry of the Spanish-born Maria Theresa into Paris to marry Marie's beloved Louis. How she had suffered! She was brought back to earth by accidentally overhearing the lackeys gossiping about her, that the Balbases intended

104

to kidnap her and force her to enter a convent in Saragossa so that the Constable Colonna might shut her up for ever within its walls.

Greatly agitated, on a sudden impulse Marie made for the French Embassy, the residence of the Ambassador M. de Villars. His wife, a kindly woman, described this visitor - the Spanish term was a *tapada* - for Marie concealed her face with a mantilla. "She wept and asked us to have pity on her," related Madame de Villars. Suddenly the ambassador recognized her. "It is the Constabless Colonna," he said.[8] Madame de Villars thought her very beautiful, her corsage à l'Espagnole,

> "which does not conceal her shoulders either too much or too little. Too long tresses of black hair tied with a flame-coloured ribbon; the rest of her hair untidy, and badly combed; very beautiful pearls round her neck (the pearls given to her by Louis XIV) . . . beautiful teeth."

Monsieur de Villars was in an embarrassing position, knowing that he might compromise himself with the Spanish government. How difficult it was to reason with the emotional lady! He reported to King Louis:

> "Sir, I was obliged to summon the Nuncio and some ladies among her friends and after a long and difficult negotiation which lasted until midnight we brought her back with her own consent to the Marquis's (Balbases) home."

Eventually she returned to the Convent of San Domingo-El-Real.

Then to her surprise her husband came every day, paying her marked attention, "such as a lover might pay his mistress". Prince Colonna's wily object was to gain his wife's consent to transfer part of the dowry her uncle had bequeathed her to their eldest son Filippo Principe di Palliano. He wanted to marry him to the daughter of the Spanish Prime Minister the Duque de Medina Coeli. Although Colonna possessed a great deal of influence in Spain, his wealth mainly consisted in debt-encumbered estates in Italy. Marie considered Medina Coeli her enemy, but she agreed to her husband's suggestion for the sake of her son.[9] For a while she left her convent to live at her husband's Palazzo in Madrid, each of them occupying a separate wing. Despite Marie's concession to Colonna there were no indications that she had gained Medina Coeli's support. Everything seemed once again ominous to her when she received orders from Carlos II, influenced by his Prime Minister, forbidding her to leave the Palazzo Colonna without her husband's authority. She must obey him in all matters.

All the same Marie often visited the royal palace to pay court to Queen Maria Luisa to whom she had been recommended by Monsieur.

The French-born Queen listened sympathetically to Marie as she poured out her troubles. She was about seventeen and possessed much of the grace, charm and vivacity of her mother Henriette d'Angleterre Duchesse d'Orléans, Monsieur's first wife, who had died so tragically ten years before. It was her misfortune as a pleasurse-loving sensual girl to be married to Carlos II[10] almost an imbecile and sexually impotent. His jaw was so deformed that he was incapable of masticating his food, forcing him to swallow it in large lumps and wrecking his digestion in the process.[11] His chief diversion was the chase, particularly the hunting and killing of wolves, but he shared a love of music with his wife. One thing is clear that the wretched Carlos, despite his health, had ardently wanted to marry Maria Luisa, Louis XIV's niece. Unlike her mother, the enchanting Madame of France (Charles II of England's Minette), the young queen was neither intellectual nor clever, and did not possess any flair for politics.

Maria Luisa proved a staunch friend to Marie Colonna, taking her side against her husband. She made the Prime Minister Duque de Medina Coeli give his solemn promise that no violence would be used against the Princess Colonna or harm befall her while she, the Queen, was absent at the Escurial.[12] As soon as the Queen departed, Medina Coeli and Balbases acted most treacherously in obtaining an order from the Junta, whom Carlos II had appointed to settle the marital disputes between the Colonnas, to have her confined in a fortress.

One night about a week after the Queen's departure, Marie was lying on her bed when a violent knocking on her door disturbed her. She could hear Don Garcia de Medrano, a member of the

106

King's Council, informing her that he had an order from the King to take her to the Alcazar of Segovia, a grim fortress not far from Madrid. After Marie refused to open the door, Don Garcia's officers had no difficulty in forcing it. Seizing a little bedside knife, which happened to be there, she tried to defend herself against the brutal attack of one of the officers, cutting his hand. Then they all flung themselves upon the half-naked lady, carrying her to a coach, to be taken to the Alcazar of Segovia. There she was thrown into a bare, draughty room in which there was not even a fire, although it was almost winter.

Marie Princess Colonna reached the lowest peak of her misfortunes during that icy winter 1680-1681, to be confined there for almost four months, badly fed and attended only by the faithful Moréna and another woman. De Villars, the French ambassador, thought it extraordinary that a woman of birth such as Marie Colonna, accused of no crime, should be treated in such a brutal way. He was convinced that it was to satisfy the animosity of the Balbases.[13]

The Queen showed Medina Coeli her anger, but there was very little she could do for the present to thwart the all-powerful Prime Minister. When the Marquis de Villars wrote King Louis whether he required him to take some action, there was no reply. Only two visitors were allowed to see her, Maria Luisa's Confessor and her friend Monsignor Mellini the Papal Nuncio, who did not fail to inform the Spanish Court of her wretched condition. The Queen then sent her Confessor to the Constable Colonna to protest strongly about the way he had treated his wife.

Forced at last to act, Lorenzo Colonna made Marie an extraordinary proposal. She might leave her prison in the Alcazar, provided she agreed to enter the Convent of the Conception in Madrid as a novice and three months later take her vows. Marie eager to leave the hated Alcazar was willing to agree to any conditions. She knew, however, that she had no vocation for the religious life and was determined never to take the vows. Nobody took very seriously Lorenzo Colonna's decision to become a monk at the same time.

At forty Marie was as beautiful as she had been at twenty, but her experiences had aged her greatly. She was always the great lady, still capable of displaying arrogance if something displeased her, but something in her spirit had broken.

She returned to Madrid February 15th 1681 and entered the Convent of the Conception, extremely depressed. Refusing to see her husband, she poured out her troubles to her sons. The Marquis de Villars described her arrival in a letter:

> "The Constabless Colonna arrived early on Saturday . . . the nuns received her at the door with tapers and all the ceremonial which is usual on such occasions, then she was conducted to the choir where she assumed the dress of a novice with a very modest demeanour . . . the dress is pretty and rather coquettish, the convent commodious."[14]

Pope Innocent XI was prepared to offer many concessions to Lorenzo Colonna, allowing him to dispense with the customary vows of chastity and poverty, and the obligation of making pilgrimages to the Holy Land so that his professed desire to become a monk was a farce. He was quite content to wear the Grand Cross of the Hospital of St. John without being subjected to any discipline.

Finally Marie refused to take her vows, unwilling to wear her religious dress. According to Madame d'Aulnoy's gossip:

> "She wore petticoats of gold and silver brocade under her woollen robe, threw aside her veil, and arranged her hair à la Espagnole with ribbons of all colours."

She now resumed her friendly relations with Queen Maria Luisa, who often visited her to take her for drives in her carriage, being very attached to her. Carlos, too, received her most graciously at Court. Fortune once again seemed to smile upon her.

During the early spring (1686), however, Marie's malignant enemy Balbases succeeded in influencing the Abbess of the Convent of the Conception against her. One evening after she had attended a magnificent reception given by the Admiral of Castile for the King and Queen, the Abbess annoyed that Madame Colonna returned to the Convent at such irregular hours, refused to admit her. Finding her quite relentless, Marie appealed to Carlos, who ordered the Abbess to admit the lady. At first she refused to obey the King, saying that she and her nuns wished for an interview with His Majesty to give their reasons. This richly amused Carlos, who burst out laughing, saying: "I shall be very much amused to see this procession of nuns who should come chanting 'Libera nos, Domine, de la Condestable'. (Free us, Lord, from the Constabless). The nuns wisely obeyed the King's orders.

The Pope soon realized that it was unwise for the Princess Colonna to remain in the convent and was sensible enough to order her release. Her husband also was forced to give Marie complete liberty, knowing that Carlos and Maria Luisa would oppose a further term of imprisonment in the Alcazar of Segovia.

Marie having the best brain of the Mancini sisters now became a highly respected personality in Madrid society. Her life became much easier and she lived for a time in a little house in the garden of the Duque de Medina Coeli with whom she was now reconciled.

CHAPTER X

Legal Action

Hortense throughout her life was usually so gay and lively, but after Charles II's death a morbid strain grew in her. With the tragic death of her Swedish lover she had known heart-rending sorrow, but Charles's death made her think of her own. She tried to convince herself of survival in the after life and would discuss the problem with a new friend, Madame de Beauclair. If she were to die before her, would she give her some sign or proof that she was still alive? Madame de Beauclair predeceased Hortense and it is related that her spirit appeared before the Duchesse Mazarin on one occasion. If Hortense had lived in the nineteenth or twentieth century, she might well have been attracted to spiritualism, attending seances with the object of communicating with discarnate spirits. This morbid mood did not last.

Occasionally she told friends she wanted to return to France, but Louis XIV had been influenced by the Duc Mazarin to discontinue paying her pension and she was largely dependent on the generosity of James II. He continued to pay her the pension granted her by his brother. Another consideration swayed her to stay in England. Surrounded by friends and admirers in London, she had a host of enemies at the French Court.

Hortense had not lost her political importance altogether, for a French diplomat, Bonrepos, wrote to his Foreign Minister, the Marquis de Seignelay, in February 1686 nearly two years before the Revolution, reminding him of the Duchesse Mazarin, now living in the little village of Chelsea in the country:

> "I cannot give you a better idea of the drollness of this Court, than by telling you that the two principal ministers (Laurence Hyde Earl of Rochester and Robert Spencer Earl of Sunderland) make it their main occupation to secure this woman's allegiance."[1]

It is more likely that these politicians enjoyed Hortense's society and courted her for that reason.

During July 1687 she received a welcome visitor, her own younger sister Marianne the Duchesse de Bouillon. Marianne was undergoing one of her periodical disgraces, having again offended King Louis. Thinking that a prolonged visit to her sister might restore her tarnished reputation, she came to London. There Hortense confided in her sister she could not leave England without paying her debts.

Both sisters now using St. Evrémond as an intermediary, tried to persuade La Fontaine, whose patron was Marianne, to come over to England. However, the poet, though surely tempted, felt too old and infirm in health to undertake such a tiring journey. He sent St. Evrémond a graceful poem in which he praised the Duchesse Mazarin's exquisite beauty and vivacity, but his first loyalty was always to Marianne. St. Evrémond truly idolized Hortense, but he was magnanimous enough to pay tribute to the Duchesse de Bouillon as well. There was a kind of contest between the two poets to determine which of their adored ladies was the fairest. For this purpose La Fontaine suggested jocularly to St. Evrémond they should sally forth as if to joust in a tournament. This friendly rivalry amused the sisters rather than causing them the slightest jealousy.

In praising Hortense's beauty, La Fontaine does not refrain from mentioning her 'esprit', that quick intelligence so characteristic of all the Mancinis. Here are several verses of his best poem about Hortense:

> 'Hortense eut du ciel en partage
> La Grâce, la beauté, l'esprit,
>   ce n'est pas tout:
> Les qualities du coeur
>   ce n'est pas tout encore
> Pour mille autres appas le monde
>   entier l'adore
> Depuis l'un jusqu'à l'autre bout[2] . . .

Hortense and Marianne were among the sixty-seven people in that crowded, stifling room in St. James's Palace in June 1688 when Mary of Modena, James's Papist Queen, gave birth to an infant prince. He was to be christened James Francis Edward, and destined to pass almost all his life in exile.

Sir Winston Churchill in a famous speech in the early days of the 1939-1945 war said:

> "History with its flickering lamp stumbles along the trail of the past trying to reconstruct its scenes, to revive its echoes and to kindle with pale gleams the passion of former days."[3]

Never was this more true of those dramatic days before the Revolution when James II was forced by his arbitrary actions to flee the country after sending his Queen and infant Prince of Wales to France. Those who so glibly call it "glorious", seldom pause to consider the treachery of politicians and others rendering it possible.

Since she held Papist sympathies Hortense was again in considerable jeopardy. With the advent of the Prince of Orange now William III and Mary II (James's daughter by Anne Hyde) to the throne, Hortense's fortunes were adversely affected. At first she lost all her pension, then eventually owing to the intercession of her many influential friends her pension of £2,000 was partly restored by William III. However, her relationship with the exiled Queen made her an object of suspicion to the Protestant party now in power. Once again she thought seriously of leaving England for France, knowing that behind the scenes attempts were being made to banish her abroad. When Marianne Duchesse de Bouillon wanted to return to France, William thoughtfully put his own yacht at her disposal.

His encounter with another Mancini sister, the Princess Colonna, when he was Prince of Orange was very curious, for he met her by chance at Blaetsum when she was running away from her Italian husband.[4]

Meanwhile the Duc Mazarin made frantic efforts to force his wife to return to him. Whether his pleas were sincere or not, it is difficult to say, but Hortense certainly did not believe in their sincerity. However, there was some force in his arguments. Now that the Crown had been seized by a foreign and Protestant usurper,

112

and the rightful sovereigns were in exile, she no longer had a valid excuse to remain in England. He argued that while her cousin the Queen still reigned he had made no objections to her remaining by her side, particularly as he was aware that James was attempting to convert his subjects to the true faith. One rather suspects that Hortense was amused when he wrote that her very soul was in danger and that he could not tolerate her remaining any longer in this Protestant sink of perdition.

Madame de Sévigné's opinion of the Duc Mazarin is absolutely different to that of the Duc de Saint-Simon. She wrote her daughter (August 13th 1689):

"There is no accounting for the extravagancy of this man; he is mad, and dresses like a beggar; devotion has quite turned his brain. We were willing to persuade him to send for his wife from England, where she is in danger of being expelled or perverted, and where she remains with the King's enemies. He always says she shall come with him; with him, good god! let us say with St. Evremond, that she is dispersed from common rules and that we see her justification when one sees M. de Mazarin."

Hortense answered her husband that she was saddled with debts and that her creditors would not allow her to leave England without payment. If her husband would settle her debts, she might consider the advisability of returning to France. She was writing in 1689 at a time when she no longer received her English pension, obliging her to borrow from her friends.

The Duchesse Mazarin could no longer afford to live in St. James's and during 1692 she moved to Kensington Square, to one of the new houses then in course of construction situated delightfully in the midst of fields. Kensington Square was built to house the courtiers attending William III when in residence in Kensington Palace. A strong tradition exists that Hortense lived for about two years in Number 11, a house that still retains its original panelling. While the Court was at Kensington most of the houses were inhabited by various ambassadors and "persons of quality" according to one authority Faükner, about 40 carriages were kept by residents in the neighbourhood. Later she moved to a small house belonging to Lord Cheyne in Paradise Row in Chelsea, then a small village with about a thousand inhabitants.

Eventually convinced that Hortense had not the slightest intention of returning to France, the Duc Mazarin appealed to the Council of State asking them to take away all her rights under the marriage settlement unless she would agree to return to France within a certain time. To present his case as favourably as possible, Mazarin employed a brilliant advocate named Erard, but gave him express instructions not to cast aspersions on his wife's virtue, a curious prohibition for it put Erard at some disadvantage. Hortense believed that her husband's real object was to gain absolute control over the Mazarin fortune. What is clear, however, is that the Duc had never lost his affection for Hortense, though the marked sadistic trait in his strange character made him want to hurt her. His motives were mixed making him strongly resentful that she opposed his wishes. He wrote during September 1689 that he was bringing the action solely in her interests,

> "as the greatest proof I could give her of an enduring affection for her, so that she can be cured of a sort of spiritual gangrene of which she herself is not conscious, but which the wise men of this world would judge mortal."[5]

Erard in presenting his case emphasized that their marriage for nearly seven years had been happy[6] and that heaven had blessed the union with several children. In reality Hortense in her good-natured way had at first too readily consented to the most outrageous demands. The advocate blamed the Duc's brother-in-law, Philippe Duc de Nevers, for instigating the quarrels between husband and wife and for being mainly culpable for ruining their marriage. Monsieur de Mazarin had the misfortune to displease Monsieur le Duc (Nevers) he alleged, insisting that his motives were owing to a natural antipathy or caused by Never's anger and resentment that his uncle the Cardinal had not made him his sole heir. There may well be some truth in this, for Mademoiselle de Montpensier (La Grande Mademoiselle) corroborates it, referring to Philippe de Never's resentment and disappointment at not being

114

created his uncle's heir.[7] However, it is unlikely that Nevers was discontented with what he had been bequeathed, taking into account his lazy and rather easy-going nature. He certainly would not have welcomed the responsibility of superintending such a vast estate. Cardinal Mazarin was well aware of that. Her brother's attitude was a sort of amused contempt, a mockery of Armand Mazarin.

For his part Hortense's husband was furiously jealous of the intimate relations between brother and sister, causing him to accuse his brother-in-law of vile things. Erard maintained that the Duchesse Mazarin was entirely under his evil influence. She had arranged a communicating door to be built between the adjoining wall of the Hôtel de Nevers (where her brother lived) and her own apartment in the Palais Mazarin by which she would leave at all hours of the day and night.[8] Hortense expressly denied this in her Mémoires, maintaining that the door had been walled up by her husband during her first absence from his house.

The advocate also accused her of removing by this means a lot of plate and jewelry, their joint property. His purpose was to justify the Duc's conduct to the Council of State, emphasizing Mazarin's honesty (honnêtetés) and consideration for his wife. Hardly credible when we are mindful that he was in the habit of taking his wife to wretched, primitive inns in the country. Erard regarded as frivolous the Duchesse's excuse that her debts were responsible for preventing her from leaving England. The Duc Mazarin had sent large sums to her during her first years in England (1676 onwards). He had only stopped sending her the money when Charles II paid her a pension. In any case, he argued, since the late King had borrowed money from Cardinal Mazarin during his exile, the pension was paid from the Mazarin estate.

Erard's attack on the England of William and Mary was typical of the attitude of France at this period. He alludes to Madame Mazarin preferring a heretic country such as England to France, eloquently comparing the two countries:

"England on fire, the theatre of revolt and heresy, to France peaceful, flourishing and Catholic: the Court of an usurper William III to that of the most just and of the greatest Prince on earth" (Louis XIV)

115

Since the Parliament in the early reign of William and Mary had wanted to banish her from the country, it is extremely unlikely that William would have put any obstacle in her way of returning to France, especially as he had already allowed the Duchesse de Bouillon to leave the country on one of his yachts. "Never was there a woman who has more deserved to be deprived of her dowry and of her covenants," Erard exclaimed.

He referred to the Duchesse's causes of complaint against her husband, his jealousy, his excessive devotion and his extravagance. With regard to his alleged jealousy, demanded Erard,

> "How can you accuse a man of this fault who has not the slightest suspicion today of your virtues and who offers to take you back?" (This is incredible since the Duc must have known of Hortense's immorality.)

> "As to his excessive devotion, if only Hortense would agree to return to him, she would discover that it had mellowed with the passage of time. How dare the Duchesse accuse her husband of extravagance. She who told you that she has not been able to subsist, alone, without a carriage, with 2000 écus pension that she has always received from the King of England."

When Erard asserted that the Duc's fortune was still intact, including movable property, Sachot the Duchesse's able advocate interrupted his opponent to point out that the famous statues (destroyed by the Duc) could hardly be considered intact. To this Erard retorted: Was his learned friend insinuating that Madame Mazarin had left her husband solely because of the mutilation of the statues?

Finally the Duc's counsel asked that the Council of State should order the Duchesse Mazarin to return to her husband within a reasonable time to be decided by themselves. If she refused to agree to these terms, all her rights under her marriage settlement must be forfeited.

Even St. Evrémond was impressed by Erard's ability in presenting his case. Although his arguments were unsound (manque de bonnes raisons), he made up for the weakness of his case by his capability and quickness of perception. This opinion is expressed in a letter to the Marquis de Saissac to whom he wrote on her behalf.[9] Referring to another letter to the same nobleman, St. Evrémond asks Hortense to give a thousand compliments to the Duke of St. Albans, Nell Gwyn's son.

The Duchesse's counsel Sachot pleaded very eloquently on her behalf, relying for the most part on a Factum, a written answer to be read by the Court. St. Evrémond had taken enormous trouble to supply the requisite information needed to support her case. The pleadings mention the pension granted to Hortense by Charles II during 1677, and the Duc Mazarin's annoyance because of the King's generosity. He had sent one of his gentlemen, Le Sieur L'Anneau, to England to tell Charles that the Duchesse's receipts were invalid,[10] reminding the King that he had borrowed heavily from the Cardinal during his exile, and the money ought therefore to revert to him. Charles had merely smiled, saying that he did not intend to take receipts from the lady. In any case he had not admitted owing any debts.

Despite Sachot's valiant efforts on her behalf, the Council after six audiences decided in favour of Hortense's husband. They decreed that she must give a detailed list of her debts within one month.

After three months she was ordered to return to France and to repair to the Convent of Chaillot for six months. Then she must return to her husband's house. If she refused to comply with any of these conditions, all her rights in the Mazarin property would be surrendered. So, Erard's powerful advocacy finally clinched the verdict of the Court.

Hortense did not make the slightest attempt to obey the decree, preferring life in England with her many friends to that in France with her husband, never possessing any confidence that Armand Mazarin would abide by his promises. Unfortunately she was quite incapable of restraining her extravagance, and if it had not been for her influential and helpful friends she would have fallen into the clutches of her creditors.[11] A few unpleasant people clamoured for her to be consigned in a debtor's prison.

Despite her troubles, for many years Hortense and St. Evrémond were fairly frequent guests at Ralph Montagu's lovely palace
Boughton in Northamptonshire, today owned by the Duke of
Buccleuch. There they would spend delightful hours in the gardens,
looking at the pike in the lakes, and eating with relish Hortense's
favourite truffles at dinner.

She was one of those rare women who preserve their beauty
and grace to the end, deeply aware of it for she wrote to St. Evrémond: "Never have I felt better, never have I been more beautiful."

St Evrémond's intimate woman friend Ninon de Lenclos, told
him in early 1699 that every visitor from London to Paris spoke
enthusiastically about the Duchesse's beauty, in much the same way
as they extolled the loveliness of her granddaughter Mademoiselle de
Bellefonds, "which is now in the bud". This was the child of Mary
Olympe, one of Hortense's daughters.

Despite Hortense's peevishness, her unpredictable moods, and
bad temper, partly caused by her too free drinking of whisky,
absinthe and white wine, life without her was worthless to St.
Evrémond. By the spring of 1699 she was £7,000 in debt, but to
please her when she fell ill he would bring her little presents of
butter and made-up dishes. He gives us a glimpse of his unhappiness
and exasperation in his verses:

> 'Seigneur, Seigneur, donne-moi patience,
> Qu'on à de mal a servir Dame Hortense.'[1][2]

Deserted by most of her friends and attendants, except for
the faithful Mustapha, an under-valet and of course St. Evrémond,
Hortense fell into a coma. Realizing that her end was near, he sent
for her Chaplain Father Milon so that she might receive from him
the last sacraments. St. Evrémond alone remained at her side while
life slowly ebbed from her, but she suffered no pain. Occasionally
he would dose her with brandy. Just before she died her face
assumed an unearthly transcendent beauty. John Evelyn relates in
his diary (July 11th 1699) that she was reported to have hastened
her death by strong spirits.

Having been informed of his mother's desperate state, her son
the Marquis de la Meilleraye and her sister Marianne Duchesse de

118

Bouillon, set out from Calais to Dover, but they disembarked only to hear that Hortense had died at eight o'clock on the morning of July 2nd. After rapidly coming to a decision, they returned to France to tell the Duc Mazarin the tragic news.

St. Simon relates that all the Duchesse's property, including her personal goods, were seized by her creditors after her death. She left little except her personal debts and her animals. A letter from Sir J. Stanley to the Duke of Shrewsbury, a statesman during the reign of William and Mary, indicates that the Duchesse Mazarin was saddled with debts. He wrote:

> "I send your Grace a warrant for furniture for the King's yacht, by his order. One for demanding five pieces of tapestry formerly lent to Madame Mazarin, which the man who has them in keeping says he will deliver upon such an order."[13]

St. Evrémond wrote to his friend the Marquis de Canaples that he had need of the tenderness of his friend and of the strength of his spirit to console himself.[14] Hortense had only paid back half of the eight hundred pounds she had borrowed from him. The old man, though absolutely disconsolate, had no thought of returning to France. "Besides what can I do in France?" he asked Canaples. "Where to hide myself? Often ill, always frail, decrepit." His life without Hortense had no purpose.

Ninon Mademoiselle de Lenclos hastened to comfort him. "What a great loss you have sustained, Monsieur," she wrote him,

> "if we were not to be lost ourselves, we cannot even be comforted. I heartily sympathize with you. You have just lost an amiable commerce in a foreign country. What can one do to retrieve such a misfortune? Those who live a long time are liable to see their friends die. After this, your spirit, your philosophy will serve to sustain you. I have felt this death as if I had had the honour of Madame Mazarin's acquaintance. She has thought of me in her sufferings. I was touched with that goodness, and her being so cherished by you, made me attached to her. There is no remedy for this

misfortune, nor is there one against which happens to our poor bodies. Take care of yours."[15]

Ralph Montagu, who had been such an intriguer at the Court of Charles II, occasionally entertained St. Evrémond at Boughton, trying to take his mind off his great sorrow by talking gaily as they walked round the gardens feeding the carp. At dinner, however, despite his desire to show a brave face, the pathetic old man sobbed bitterly when the first course, truffles, was served, reminding him unbearably of his lost Hortense. He thought that she might still be alive had she conserved her vitality. She would heed the advice of nobody, only intent on living with her usual reckless abandon as if still a young girl. It was not in her nature to submit to the inevitable changes that befall mankind. St. Evrémond's grief was more that of a widower than a devoted friend.

That strange man her real widower, the Duc Mazarin, mourned his wife in his own peculiar, eccentric way. On August 13th 1699 he had her body conveyed to France, being present at the Church of Notre-Dame-de-Liesse to receive it. Among those who escorted her on her last journey were her executors Lord Montagu, Lord Feversham and, of course, St. Evrémond and Mustapha, her Moorish attendant.

Though separated from her for more than thirty years, the Duc Mazarin could not bear to be parted from his wife, so he had her body put in a coffin and carried restlessly about from one estate to another, from Vincennes to Brittany, and from Bourbon to Alsace. Later Hortense's body was removed to be buried in the tomb of her uncle Cardinal Mazarin in the Church of the Collège des Quatre Nations in Paris.

St. Evrémond survived her by about four years, dying on September 11th 1703 at the age of ninety. It is fitting that this illustrious wit, poet and philosopher should be buried among his fellows in Poet's Corner, Westminster Abbey, and there is a monument with an inscription to his memory there. The Jacobite Dean of Westminster, Atterbury, mentions him rather scathingly, but the monument was erected by one of the prebendaries, Dr. Birch, because of St. Evrémond's old acquaintance with Edmund Waller. I can never pass the memorial without reflecting on the strangeness of life on this planet and remembering the beautiful, unique woman who with all her faults had inspired some of his best work.

How strange are the threads of destiny. Four descendants of Hortense and her only son Paul Jules, Duc de la Meilleraye in turn became mistresses of Louis XV, great-grandson of Le Roi Soleil, possessing as he did, as a young man and later much of the sensuality of Louis XIV. The dukedom of Mazarin became extinct in 1738 on the death of Gui Paul Jules, the son of Paul Jules, but his daughter Armande Félicité married the Marquis de Nesle, the father of Louis XV's four early mistresses. Perhaps he set a bad example being a notorious gambler. The first sister was Mme. de Mailly, who loved the King as Louise de la Vallière had once loved his great-grandfather. When Louis tired of the vivacious lady he transferred his affections to her younger sister the Duchesse de Vintimille for whom he bought a pleasant hunting-box on the Seine. The most disagreeable of these sisters was the Duchesse de Châteauroux, a scheming, brazen woman, who Louis eventually recognized as his *maîtresse en titre*.[16] A Montespan rather than a Vallière, coached by her cousin the Duc de Richelieu, First Gentleman of the bedchamber, an experienced rake, the Duchesse used all her arts to entice the susceptible Louis. These sisters with one exception did not inherit the beauty and the unique charm of their ancestress Hortense Mancini. Her namesake Hortense Félicité, a beautiful and virtuous girl, happily married to a loving, but possessive husband, was the only one to be spared becoming Louis's mistress.

Epilogue

Olympe Comtesse de Soissons survived her sister Hortense eight years. During early 1686 she continued her wanderings, travelling to Spain probably for the purpose of trying to arrange a suitable marriage for her younger son Prince Eugène, destined to become a famous soldier. He remained a bachelor all his life. At first Marie Princess Colonna gave her sister a warm welcome, but she soon became aware of Olympe's political intrigues and strongly disapproved of them.

From the first King Carlos II took a marked dislike to Olympe, doing his utmost to prevent her visits to his Queen Maria Luisa with whom she was soon on very friendly terms. Carlos undoubtedly had been prejudiced against the Comtesse de Soissons, having heard many tales of her sinister reputation as an associate of sorceresses. On the other hand Maria Luisa liked her society, for it reminded her of her beloved France.

Both Carlos and Maria Luisa longed for an heir, but the King of Spain was unfortunate enough to suffer from a form of psychosexual impotence, making it impossible for him to achieve penetration.[1] Carlos was ardent enough in marriage, but his unnatural sexual relations with his wife resulted in frayed nerves, sudden tempests and mutual recrimination.

During 1688 Louis XIV's ambassador at the Spanish Court was the young Comte de Rébenac, an emotional rather opinionated man, very attached in a chivalrous way to his Queen. His letters to King Louis are deeply arresting, providing a vivid picture of Olympe's intrigues. Writing on October 7th he says:

> "The King of Spain was warned against her, he accused her of sorcery and I learn that some days ago he conceived the idea that had it not been for a spell which she had cast over him, he would have had children."[2]

It so happened that a convenient opportunity for getting rid of Olympe now occurred. After a noisy brawl between some Spaniards and Madame de Soisson's servants it was intimated to her that it would be as well for her to retire to Flanders, where she would be given the estate of Terveuren for life. Much agitated and unwilling to agree to this plan, Olympe sought an interview with Maria Luisa, who merely advised the lady to obey the King's wishes.[3]

Both Louis XIV and the Comte de Rébenac were well aware that the Comtesse de Soissons, vindictive by nature, harboured strong resentment against the King of France and was working against his interests.

The Court of Spain was divided at this period into two hostile factions, the Austrian and the French parties. The head of the Austrian party was the Graf von Mansfeld, a friend of Olympe's and the Spanish Prime Minister the Conde de Oropesa. Arrayed against the Austrian party was the less formidable French faction with its champion the Queen doing her utmost to dissuade King Carlos from attaching himself to the powerful Cabal forming against him. Though after eight years she had lost her ascendancy over her husband, who disliked all Frenchmen, she still possessed influence with Carlos, who had some affection for her. Working against Maria Luisa were her own Austrian-born mother-in-law Mariana of Austria (Philip IV of Spain second Queen), Mansfeld the scheming Austrian Ambassador, Oropesa the Prime Minister and most of the Council.

Louis XIV instructed Rébenac to keep a close watch on the Comtesse de Soissons, though he was not to hold any communication with her. "Endeavour," he wrote October 23rd 1688,

> "notwithstanding, to keep yourself always well informed of her intrigues, in order to give on this subject to the Queen the counsel most comfortable to her interests."

Meanwhile, according to Rébenac, Olympe after falsely suspecting Queen Maria Luisa of a share in seeking her exile in Flanders, was reconciled to her.

The ambassador described to King Louis Olympe's life in Madrid, where she kept open house, "entertaining all persons who desire to come there from four o'clock in the evening up to two or three hours after midnight." He mentions the gluttony of the Spaniards, "stuffing themselves with food, professional gormand-izers", but it is evident most people of good repute, including grandees, avoided Olympe's society.

Carlos extremely superstitious by nature was tortured by his dread of evil spirits, and his dislike of the Comtesse de Soissons became an obsession. It has never been satisfactorily explained why Olympe should resort to such a diabolical device as to cast a spell over the King to thwart his desire for an heir to the throne,[4] if this were true. However, she now burnt with resentment against Louis. One of his greatest mistakes was to deny Olympe's son Eugène Prince of Savoy the opportunity of a career in the French army during February 1683, possibly because he considered the young man of twenty lacked military promise, more likely owing to Louis's Secretary of State for War, Louvois's hatred of Olympe Soissons for rejecting a possible marriage between one of her daughters and his son. Eugène turned instead to Leopold Holy Roman Emperor since 1659. As a soldier of genius he fought in his armies against France.

Rebénac the French ambassador in a curious despatch written on December 23rd 1688 alleged that Carlos made use of the serv-ices of a Dominican monk, who was reported to possess the power of exorcising evil spirits. "The ceremony is horrible, Sir," wrote the diplomat, "car le roy et la reine devoient estre déshabillés touts nuds".[5] The monk in vestments must perform the exorcisms, but in an infamous manner . . . The Queen has been violently pers-ecuted by the King to agree to this, but has absolutely refused to consent. Rebénac alleged that he had received an anonymous letter that if Maria Luisa agreed to the monk's suggestion for hav-ing children, she would be lost. According to the ambassador's information it was all a cunning plot of the Conde de Oropesa the Prime Minister to prove that the Queen was bewitched before marriage so that it could be made void. It seems likely, however that Rebénac's quixotic zeal on his Queen's behalf made him prone to distort the truth. If Oropesa had really concocted such a plot, as indecent as it was horrible, he might have been charged by the Inquisition with serious heretical practices.

Rébenac usually refers to Marie Colonna as the Constabless when writing to Louis XIV, for instance on October 7th 1688, commending her for not meddling in any intrigues, unlike her sister Olympe.

> "She has many influential friends, and although she has not quarrelled with her sister the Comtesse de Soissons, no one was so much rejoiced as was she at the order that had been given the latter to withdraw."

In his correspondence the ambassador often refers to a mysterious person "devoted to the interests of France whom he often consults", but he does not mention her name. Lucien Perey in his biography of the Princess Colonna opines that the person alluded to is undoubtedly Marie.

In his despatch of January 16th 1689 Rebenac mentions that he has given a portrait of King Louis set with diamonds "to the person for whom Your Majesty intended it and that it has been received with respect and gratitude." It would have consoled Marie for all the rebuffs she had received from the King. How she would have cherished it. Rébenac would have benefited from her astute advice.

During the last months of her short life the Queen of Spain expressed fears that her life was in danger, knowing that deadly enemies such as the Comte de Mansfeld, the Emperor's ambassador in Madrid, and the Prime Minister Oropesa wanted to be rid of her. Even her weak-minded husband Carlos II had been warned that it was intended to poison the Queen, and warned her to have her food tasted. Maria Luisa sometimes wrote to her uncle King Louis. In one pathetic letter she tells him:

> "I cannot hide from Your Majesty that my life is in danger, since my enemies will snatch it away if their present designs fail."

According to Madame de la Fayette she even wrote to her father Monsieur, asking for an antidote against poison. The Duc d'Orléans

sent her one, but it arrived too late, after her death. Her early pop-
ularity was no more for the Spanish people blamed her most un-
justly for not giving Carlos an heir to the throne.

Saint-Simon was to write thirty years later accusing Olympe
Comtesse de Soissons of the crime of poisoning Maria Luisa, but
the Queen's contemporaries make no mention of Olympe in this
connection, nor does Rébenac, who certainly would have shown
no reluctance to point the finger of suspicion at Olympe if evidence of her guilt existed. Saint-Simon's account is prejudiced and
is very unlikely to be the truth. He relates:

> "It appears that in the end the Countess came occasionally
> after dinner to the Queen's apartments by a secret staircase,
> and saw her only in the King's presence. These visits re-
> doubled and always with repugnance on the part of the
> King. He had asked of the Queen as a favour never to taste
> anything that he had not eaten or drunk before, because he
> was well aware that it was intended to poison her. The
> weather was hot, milk is scarce in Madrid. The Queen ex-
> pressed a desire for some and the Countess . . . boasted of
> some that was excellent, which she promised to bring her in
> a glass. It is asserted that it was prepared at the Comte de
> Mansfeld's house. The Comtesse de Soissons brought it to
> the Queen, who swallowed it at a draught and died shortly
> afterwards."

Saint-Simon's account is wholly inaccurate when he alleged that
Olympe fled from the Palace immediately the Queen had drunk
the milk and managed to escape from Spain. In reality she remained in Spain until May 1689 when Carlos II ordered her expulsion,
possibly suspecting her of the crime.

Three months before on February 8th Maria Luisa sustained
an accident while engaged in her favourite exercise on horseback,
but she forbade her ladies to mention it. Her diet was certainly
very curious. She ate broth made of veal gristle, chicken and meat
frozen in four pounds of snow, oysters with lemon and she was
especially partial to gooseberry fool and Chinese oranges. It was,
perhaps, hardly surprising that in the early hours of February 10th

she awoke with violent stomach ache and diarrhoea. Her doctors diagnosed Cholera morbus, applying the usual remedies for her failing heart, such as emulsion of opium with cordial water, extract of egg yolk and triacil water, but to no avail. At first she declared she had been poisoned, like her mother, Henriette Duchess of Orléans, Charles II of England's sister. Hortense's friend Ralph Montagu, as a young ambassador to France, was present when she died at Saint-Cloud, nineteen years ago after drinking chicory water. However, Maria Luisa told Rébenac when he was eventually allowed to see her that she was certainly mistaken. They were both aged twenty-six. Ralph Montagu always declared that Madame (Henriette-Anne) had been poisoned and Rébenac was convinced also that his Queen had been poisoned.

A. Legrelle, an eminent documentary French historian, after closely examining the medical reports of the doctors, who performed the autopsy on the diseased Queen believes in the probability that Maria Luisa was poisoned.[6] This conclusion is hotly disputed by the Spanish historian the Duque de Maura, who accuses Legrelle of a natural enmity to all Cosas de Espana.[7] That most of the Queen of Spain's contemporaries such as Madame de la Fayette her own step-mother, Charlotte Elizabeth of Bavaria and even probably Louis XIV himself (according to the French historian Dangeau) believed she had been poisoned is suggestive, but does not prove anything. Both Count Mansfeld and the Conde de Oropesa had motives for the crime and suspicion fastened on them. I believe in their guilt.

Also suspected of poisoning the Queen, Olympe Comtesse de Soissons continued her wandering life, travelling to Germany, Portugal, Holland and Belgium. Whilst in The Hague she had a curious encounter with King William III. Olympe's coffee parties were very popular, but the King expressed some annoyance when she never invited him. "I do not see why I should be treated as a son of a bitch (en fils de putain)," he said, "You know what I am accused of," exclaimed Olympe. "If anything happened to you my life would not be worth an hour's purchase." On William's insistence, however, he attended one of them and he later invited her to play cards with him.[8]

During the summer of 1708 she was in Brussels where a Journal *Les Relations Véretables* mentions her son Prince Eugène

127

visiting her on one occasion when on the way to the Camp of Assche to hold a Council of War with the Duke of Marlborough.[9] By the early autumn Olympe was seriously ill and she died on October 9th. The same journal mentions her charity to the poor, but in many ways she possessed the most unattractive character of the Mancini sisters. Later that year Eugène and Marlborough shared the laurels for the important allied victory over the French, the Battle of Oudenarde. On one occasion many years earlier when undertaking a raid on Southern France with the Imperial General Count Aeneas Capraro, Eugène is alleged to have boasted to another Imperial General,

> "Didn't I say I would only return to France sword in hand? Louis exiled my mother, the Countess of Soissons, and I have just exiled thousands of his subjects by making them flee from their houses and country."

In his unforgiving nature he resembled his mother.

Marie preferred living most of her later life in Spain, where she had many friends. When her husband the Prince Colonna, a hearty penitent, died in Rome April 15th 1689 he deeply regretted that he had treated his wife with such harshness and cruelty. Asking for her forgiveness, he commended Marie to the care of their sons. Human nature is always strange and unpredictable. Despite their long estrangement Marie reproached herself bitterly for not returning to her husband three years before when he had offered to take her back. She was absolutely desolate, refusing to see few visitors except her favourite son Don Carlo, who arrived in Madrid bearing his father's betrothal ring, bequeathed to her.[10]

In Madrid Marie was on very friendly terms with Maria Anna of Newburg, the new German Queen of Carlos II, though Marie's own sympathies naturally remained pro French. Highly regarded in Spain, she spoke Spanish fluently and foreign ambassadors eagerly attended her receptions. Poor Carlos II, no more capable of providing his kingdom with an heir on his second marriage than on his first, died in 1700, having signed a will bequeathing Spain, Spanish dominions, the Netherlands and other territories to Louis XIV's grandson Philippe Duc d'Anjou. He was the last of the Spanish Habsburgs.

Philip V was at first recognized as King of Spain by most of the governments of Europe, but during May 1702 in London, The Hague and Vienna, war was declared against France, the War of the Spanish succession.

Maria Anna, widowed Queen of Carlos II, was exiled to Toledo during January 1702, but the Princess Colonna always faithful to her friends accompanied her there. She made attempts to reconcile Maria Anna with the new King of Spain and was present when they met. Philip was very gracious to Marie. Perhaps he reminded her of King Louis in his youth, for he was handsome, but unlike his grandfather he was extremely uxorious, being at the same time the tyrant and the slave of the woman he married.[11]

During 1703 King Louis granted permission to Marie to visit France, but on reaching Paris she wrote her son Don Carlo that she found it greatly changed, not having been there for forty-two years. When Louis invited her to come to Versailles, she courteously declined the invitation knowing that Louis would find her physical appearance much ravaged by time. She was too proud to face a meeting after so many years.

Later Marie left for Italy where she spent her last years mostly in Rome, Florence and Venice. Her main concern now were her three sons Filippo, Don Carlo and Marc Antonio. Filippo succeeded his father as Grand Constable of Naples, Don Carlo became a Cardinal, while Marc Antonio married a former mistress of his father.

All Marie's sisters predeceased her, including Marianne Duchesse de Bouillon, who died in Paris during 1714. She was always very conscious of her own self-importance, indulging in a furious dispute with the Duchess of Hanover (the Electress Sophie), a German princess, over a question of precedence. Where he was sometimes unjust to Olympe, Saint-Simon eulogized Marianne, describing her as the Queen of Paris:

> "While at Paris from her house, all were more lowly than the grass before her . . . She preserved an air of superiority over everyone, which she knew how to apportion and to season with much skill, according to the rank of those with whom she came in contact. Her house was open from the morning . . . morning and evening she kept a splendid table; high play

went on there, and of all kinds at the same time. She was intelligent, spoke well, argued freely, and always went to the heart of anything. Intelligence and beauty sustained her, and the world accustomed itself to be governed by her."

Marianne's death was followed by that of Marie's son, the Constable of Naples, who died in her arms during November, undoubtedly a greater blow. Her brother Philippe de Nevers, husband of Diane de Thianges and father of four sons and two daughters, had died earlier in May 1707.

Marie is buried in the Church of the Holy Sepulchre in Pisa, dying in May 1715.[1][2] She chose her own epitaph.

> Maria Mancini Colonna
> Pulvis et Cinis
> Dust and Ashes

Tragic enough for the impetuous, passionate girl, who had wanted to be Queen of France.

Notes

INTRODUCTION

1. Mentioned in Patrick Morrah's *Restoration England*.
2. See page 165 Vol. I, Anthony à Wood, *Life and Times*, Oxford Historical Society, 1891-1900.
3. See Lady Antonia Fraser, *Charles II*, p. 261.
4. See *Nell Gwyn* by Bryan Bevan (1969).

CHAPTER I

1. He achieved the cardinalcy in December 1631, but never wore the cardinal's hat.
2. Madame de Motteville wrote that he certainly had grand designs based on those little girls. His indifference about them was all pure comedy.
3. Jean-Baptiste Colbert, who started his career as a valued secretary of Cardinal Mazarin.
4. See Rénee's *Les Nièces de Mazarin*, p. 257. It seems probable that he had dreamed of marrying Olympe to the King.
5. Mémoires de Madame la Duchesse Mazarin.
6. Henriette, youngest daughter of Queen Henriette now in exile at Louis XIV's Court.
7. Mémoires de Madame de Montpensier, VII, 100.
8. (Correspondence Angleterre) C.A. 71, f. 188.
   The Vagabond Duchess by Cyril Hughes Hartmann.
9. Mémoires de Mademoiselle de Montpensier, VII, 143 and seq.
10. Les illustres adventurières ou Mémoires d'Hortense et de Marie Mancini, p. 36.
11. Mémoires de Madame de Motteville sur Anne d'Autriche et se cour et une notice sure Mme. de Motteville part Saint Beuve.
12. Lucien Perey's *Le Gran Roman*, p. 256.
13. See also Philippe Erlanger's *Louis XIV*.
14. Lettres unedités du Cardinal Mazarin, publiées par M. Cheruel dans le journal général de l'instruction publiqué du 11 Octobre 1854).
15. See pages 533 and 534 Perey's *Le Roman du Grand Roi*.
16. Mémoires de La Duchesse Mazarin.
17. The old Hôtel Tubeut, the galleries erected by Mansart and dependencies adjoining Rue des Petits-Champs.
18. Mémoires de Madame Mazarin (The Duchesse Mazarin).

CHAPTER II

1. 4 Oeuvres de Saint-Evrémond, p. 264.
2. Tome 23, p. 202, edited by A. de Boislisle.
3. *The Vagabond Duchess* by Cyril Hughes Hartmann, p. 73.
4. St. Evrémond Oeuvres V. 218.
5. Journal of Olivier d'Ormesson, Tome II, pages 274, 275. Louise de la Vallière was a maid of honour to Henriette Duchesse d'Orléans.
6. P. 207, Tome 23, Mémoires de Saint-Simon.
7. *The Vagabond Duchess* by Cyril Hughes Hartmann.
8. Mémoires et Correspondence de Madame de Courcelles.

CHAPTER III

1. Many years later Monsieur Erard, Counsel for Duc Mazarin, gives the date of his wife's flight as June 13th or 14th 1667. It is incorrect.
2. Charles's letter is among the originals at the Ministère des Affaires Etrangères, Quai d'Orsay.
3. *Five Fair Sisters* by H. Noel Williams.
4. *Privileged Persons* by Hester Chapman (1966).
5. Letter published by Amédée Rénée, 'Les Nièces de Mazarin'. See also *The Vagabond Duchess* by Cyril Hughes Hartmann.
6. Lettres de Madame de Sévigné II, 84.
7. He lived from 1629-1696, the father of the future George I of England.
8. *Sophie Electress of Hanover, a personal portrait* by Maria Kroll, p. 105.
9. Today most authorities consider she died of acute peritonitis and her own state of health was always delicate.
10. Lucien Perey's *Princess Marie Colonna*.
11. Mémoires of the Duchess Mazarin.

CHAPTER IV

1. *Princess Marie Colonna* by Lucien Perey. Archives des Affaires Etrangères, Quai d'Orsay, Paris.
2. Letters of the Marchioness de Sévigné, Vol. II, with introductory essay by Madame Duclaux.
3. *Five Fair Sisters* by H. Noel Williams (1907).
4. Madame de Scudéry writing to Bussy-Rabutin, August 1672.
5. Marie Colonna's Mémoires, *La Vérité dans son Jour*.

CHAPTER V

1. *Privileged Persons* by Hester Chapman, p. 219.
2. Perey's *Marie Mancini Colonna*, pages 255 and 256; also Archives Royales de Turin Corr. dipl. Vol. LXIII, p. 337, Affaires Etrangères, Turin.
3. Le Journal d'Orlier is deposited in the royal archives in Turin, also Perey's *Marie Mancini Colonna*.
4. Pecan may mean salted or pickled.
5. March 26th 1676. British Library Mss.
6. *Charles the Second's Minette* by Bryan Bevan.
7. Fables de La Fontaine avec un nouveau commentaire litteraire et grammatical dédié au roi par CH. Nodier. La Fontaine born July 8th 1621 at Paris, died 1695 Château-Thierry.

CHAPTER VI

1. George Savile, *A Character of Charles II and political Moral Miscellaneous Thoughts and Reflections.*
2. Mémoires et Correspondence de La Marquise de Courcelles.
3. Letters of the Marquise de Sévigné to her daughter the Comtesse de Grignan, vol. IV, p. 175.
4. The picture and character of the Duchesse Mazarin.
5. Anne Hyde, the Duke of York's first wife, had died in 1671.
6. Correspondence Angleterre, Quai d'Orsay, Paris 118 f.9. Ruvigny to Louis XIV, March 12th 1676.
7. *Nell Gwyn Royal Mistress* by John Harold Wilson (1972).
8. C.A. (Correspondence Angleterre) 120 A. 17 April 15th 1676.
9. The letters of John Wilmot Earl of Rochester edited by J. Treglowne.
10. Correspondence Angleterre, CXIX, fol. 1.
11. "Kill me by not looking at me, but do not kill me with jealousy."

CHAPTER VII

1. *London Green* by Neville Braybrooke, p. 158.
2. *The Vagabond Duchess* by Cyril Hughes Hartmann.
3. *Ibid.*, Hartmann.
4. C.A. 122 f. 52 Courtin to Pomponne, January 18th 1677.
5. *Lives of the Gamesters*, Theophilus Lucas (1714).
6. Belvoir MSS, II, 34. *The Vagabond Duchess* by Cyril Hughes Hartmann.
7. *The Royal Whore* by Allen Andrews.
8. Rutland II HMC (Historical Manuscripts Commission), p. 31.
9. *The Vagabond Duchess* by Cyril Hughes Hartmann.
10. Oeuvres de St. Evrémond, 1739, V. 212.

CHAPTER VIII

1.   Hist. Mss. Comm. Report XI, II, 238; *The Vagabond Duchess* by Cyril Hughes Hartmann.
2.   Correspondence Angleterre, p. 46 f. 142; Barillon to Louis XIV.
3.   St. Evrémond, Oeuvres, 1739, V. 26.
4.   St. Evrémond, Oeuvres 1739. IV. 67; *The Vagabond Duchess* by Cyril Hughes Hartmann.
5.   St. Evrémond, Oeuvres 1739. IV. 67.
6.   A Character of Saint Evrémond, British Library.
7.   Oeuvres de St. Evrémond IV. 168 and 16.
8.   Oeuvres de St. Evrémond IV. 170; 4. 164.
9.   See Tome 24, p. 300. Jamais femme qui s'occupat moins de sa toilette.
10.   Treasury Books 1676-1679, (1685) obit Cyril Hughes Hartmann.
11.   Sidney Correspondence, II, 12.
12.   Saint Evrémond, Oeuvres IV. 176.
13.   Saint Evrémond, Oeuvres V. 141.
14.   *The Vagabond Duchess* by Cyril Hughes Hartmann.
15.   *The Vagabond Duchess* by Cyril Hughes Hartmann, p. 240.
16.   Saint Evrémond, Oeuvres IV. 270 (1739).
17.   Lucien Perey's *Marie Mancini Colonna.*
18.   Lettres de Madame de Sévigné, VII. 23.
19.   Oeuvres de St. Evrémond (1739) Tome 4, p. 194.

CHAPTER IX

1.   Madame de Sévigné to her daughter February 21st 1680. H. Noel Williams *Five Fair Sisters.*
2.   Tome 24 Mémoires de St. Simon.
3.   *Five Fair Sisters* by H. Noel Williams (1907).
4.   Voltaire's *Siècle de Louis XIV.*
5.   Tome 24. Mémoires de St. Simon.
6.   *Louis XIV*, Philippe d'Erlanger, p. 160.
7.   Lettres de Madame de Sévigné.
8.   Note 21, page 133, Mémoires de La Cour d'Espagne by Monsieur de Villars.
9.   Madame d'Aulnoy, Mémoires de la Cour d'Espagne.
10.   Son of Philip IV who had died in 1665.
11.   *Carlos the Bewitched* by John Nada (1962).
12.   Mémoires de la Cour d'Espagne by Monsieur Villars.
13.   Mémoires de la Cour d'Espagne sous le Regne de Charles II (1678-1682).
14.   *Five Fair Sisters* by H. Noel Williams.

CHAPTER X

1. *Robert Spencer Earl of Sunderland 1641-1702* by K.P. Kenyon (1958).
2. Oeuvres de St. Evrémond Tome 4, 455. Des Maizeau's English Edition. Hartmann, p. 249.
3. Winston Churchill's tribute to the late Prime Minister Nevile Chamberlain in Church House, November 12th 1940.
4. Nesca Robb's *William of Orange*, Vol. I, 287.
5. Cyril Hughes Hartmann, *The Vagabond Duchess*, p. 255.
6. Pleadings of M. Erard for Monsieur le Duc de Mazarin. Mélange Curieux des Meilleures pièces, Tome 2, 122.
7. Mémoires de Mademoiselle de Montpensier, VII, 55.
8. Mélange Curieux des Meilleures pièces (Oeuvres de St. Evremond) Tome 2, 125.
9. *Ibid.* Tome 2, 237.
10. St. Evrémond, Oeuvres 5, 202.
11. Mélange Curieux des Meilleures pièces, Tome 2, page 284.
12. Oeuvres de St. Evrémond V, 80 (1739).
13. MSS of the Duke of Buccleuch and Queensberry Vol. II, part 2, H.M.C.
14. St. Evrémond, Works, 1728, III.
15. Cyril Hughes Hartmann, *The Vagabond Duchess*, 268.
16. *Louis XV. The Monarchy in Decline* by G.P. Gooch (1956).

EPILOGUE

1. *Carlos the Bewitched* by John Nada (1960).
2. Archives des Affaires Etrangères Quai d'Orsay; H. Noel Williams, *Five Fair Sisters*.
3. Ditto.
4. In any case Carlos was incapable of having children.
5. The King and Queen must be undressed completely naked.
6. A. Legrelle, *La Mission de M. de Rébenac à Madrid et la Morte de Maria Luisa Reine d'Espagne* (Paris 1894).
7. Maura Gamizo, Duque Gabriel de, *Maria Luisa de Orleans Reina de Espana, Madrid.*
8. *William of Orange*, Nesca A. Robb, Vol. II, 325.
9. Amédée Rénée, *Les Nieces de Mazarin.*
10. *Five Fair Sisters* by H. Noel Williams.
11. *King Charles III of Spain* by Sir Charles Petrie.
12. The date of Marie's death is uncertain. Her will is dated March 30th 1706.

Index